A Western Approach to

Zen

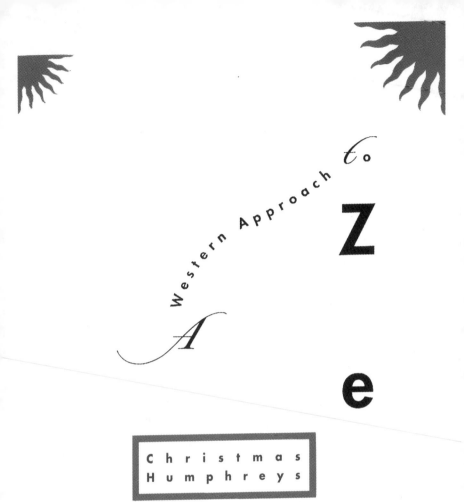

A Western Approach to Zen

Z e n

Christmas Humphreys

A publication supported by
THE KERN FOUNDATION

Quest Books

Theosophical Publishing House

Wheaton, Illinois ♦ Chennai (Madras), India

The Theosophical Publishing House
P.O. Box 270
Wheaton, IL 60189-0270

A publication of the Theosophical Publishing House,
a department of the Theosophical Society in America

Published by arrangement with George Allen and Unwin Ltd., London

Library of Congress Catalog Number 72-76428
ISBN 0-8356-0550-7

Printed in the United States of America

Dedicated
to the members
of the Zen Class of
the Buddhist Society, London

Contents

Publisher's Note

In 1971, when Christmas Humphreys—among the premier Western scholars of Buddhism of our century—wrote *A Western Approach to Zen,* he sounded a gong for the arrival of Zen and other forms of Buddhism to the West. At that time, as Humphreys lamented on an introductory page in the original edition titled "The Problem," it seemed unlikely that "a quantity of Rinzai Zen Roshis" would become resident in Europe (to say nothing of the United States) or that "a quantity of Europeans" would reach the rank of Roshi. Nor was it practical, he continued, for large numbers of Westerners to learn Japanese well and spend long years in a Japanese monastery.

"How then," he asked, "should the earnest Western student of Zen approach its goal, Zen experience, and its 'maturing' and application to daily life thereafter?"

As a substitute, Humphreys proposed a course of mind-development that could push the intellect to its limits through the contemplation of Zen mind puzzles, or koans. This course, along with wonderfully clear basic teachings on the Zen Buddhist path, is the theme of Humphreys' *A Western Approach to Zen.*

Humphreys was wrong about the Roshis, of course. Nor do Westerners need now to trek to Japan to practice regularly in a monastery or Zendo. But Humphreys' mind-development course is, if anything, more useful today than it was when he devised it as a solution to "The Problem."

As more and more Americans are drawn to the mindful simplicity of meditation, Humphreys' clear explanations and his step-by-step instructions, which guide us from Phase One "Unthink" through Phase Four "Beyond Thought," is a perfect first step on the meditative path.

These gentle meditations, he writes, waken the intuition to produce "illumined thought," preparing the mind for the direct experience of reality achieved in Zen awareness.

It is our hope that this edition will help a new generation of readers along the way toward such awareness.

Preface

The major part of this work has been compiled from notes of a course carried out in the Zen Class of the Buddhist Society. The course was first held from September 1969 to March 1970, and then, more fully and based upon a written syllabus, from September 1970 to March 1971. To help the general reader I have, however, begun this volume with a series of chapters on basic Buddhism, followed by some on the Zen School of Buddhism. Only then have I introduced a description of the course itself with an eponymous chapter on 'A Western Approach to Zen,' setting out my reasons for presenting it.

Many of the earlier chapters have appeared in various Buddhist and Theosophical magazines, notably *The Middle Way,* the journal of the Buddhist Society, and I am grateful to the editors concerned. The chapters in Parts Three and Four have been written up from notes made for the Class. 'Experiments in Zen' are reprinted from *Zen Comes West.*

I claim no authority for a single statement in the book, nor for its thesis, and because the views and suggestions therein are based on personal experience I have given few precise references for the wide range of quotation. When I am putting forward ideas which may seem strange to the Western mind I find it useful to support my contentions with the words of other more distinguished writers, but I do not suggest that even their statements have the force of authority, and the exact source of any quotation therefore seems to me unnecessary.

Quite half of these quotations come from the writing or remembered words of the late Dr. D. T. Suzuki, who died in 1966 at the age of 95. He first visited the Society in 1936, and in 1946 I spent much time with him in Japan. Thereafter I was in constant correspondence with him as his London agent and helped to publish or republish a dozen of his major works. He visited the Society many times in 1953, 1954 and 1958, and was of immense service to the Zen Class. He was to my mind the greatest Buddhist scholar with whom, in fifty years in the Buddhist field, I have come in contact, and on the subject of Zen his combination of learning and spiritual experience was unique. For me he was a master of Zen comparable with any of those whose words have come down to us, and for any proposition that I venture to advance the confirming words of the master ratify for me my own discoveries.

A few poems have been interleaved with the chapters to express in verse what I often find it easier to say that way. Other poems intended for this volume have already appeared in *Buddhist Poems* (Allen & Unwin, 1971).

I am grateful to all who have taken my original, ill-typed MS and reproduced it in intelligible prose; in particular Miss Pat Wilkinson, Miss Muriel Clarke, Mrs. Dorothy Willan and Mr. Hyde-Chambers, all of the Buddhist Society.

There remains the vexed question of diacritical marks, and the right way to set out terms in oriental languages. As for the former I advocate the minimum or none, for we must learn how to present and use these words in Western form. As for the right way to use and present such terms as must be kept, for want of an English equivalent, I have anglicized as many as possible. As Buddhists in the West increase in number we must learn the manifold meaning of these words in the original and use them to enrich our language. Many have already come to stay.

As for my wife, I have not in the forty-five years of the Society's life published a word without her careful and often amending scrutiny. The karmic responsibility for all herein remains, however, mine.

St John's Wood, 1971   T.C.H.

Introduction

This is not a clever book for clever people. It is, or is meant to be, a helpful book for ordinary people. It emanates from a Western mind living in the West that refuses to accept Zen as a Chinese/Japanese monopoly, or to regard as exclusive the Eastern approach to it.

Western mentality is complementary to that of the East, neither better nor worse but profoundly different. It follows that the Western approach to Zen will itself be different from that of China or Japan.

I believe that Zen Buddhism has something to give the West in its hour of spiritual need, something at present lacking which does not seem to be appearing in any other form.

Zen teaching defines the limits of the intellect, and demonstrates that Truth, as distinct from changing doctrine, can only be known by the use of a faculty that operates beyond the reach of thought, a power known in the East as Buddhi or Prajna and in the West as the intuition. Thought must be used until thought can go no further, but when all has been learnt 'about it and about', there remains the actual knowing, beyond description, which is pure experience for the knowing mind.

As a school of spiritual training Zen Buddhism—a term here used to include the Ch'an School of China and the Zen School of Japan— was founded in the sixth century AD to deflate the extravagance of Indian Buddhist thought and to drive the mind with earthy violence back to the origin of 'Buddhism', which is the Enlightenment achieved by Gautama the Buddha. The early masters of Ch'an sought the same personal direct attainment without scripture, ritual or formulated thought, and all Zen training is concerned with one thing only, awareness of the Absolute within the heart of man.

The West differs from the East in its emphasis on intellect. 'Below' it, in psychic perception, and 'above' it, in the intuition, Truth may be found by the few; for the many the power of thought, extroverted into the world about us or introverted in psychology to study itself, stands supreme. Whether we regret or approve this state of affairs it must be accepted as a constituent of our present civilization.

Yet the limitations of thought are becoming more and more obvious, and increasingly admitted by some of the greatest intellects of our time. As God, the Christian misunderstanding of the Absolute, fades from our conditioned consciousness, there is a growing hunger for the Beyond of which this symbol of a Saviour/Creator is quite inadequate. Increasing numbers of people are seeking in the beyond of intellect some way by which this More may be obtained. Such a way has been known to the East for twelve hundred years, and Western minds, to whom it has been patiently explained for fifty years by the late Dr D. T. Suzuki, now know a great deal about Zen Buddhism but little, alas, of Zen. This is inevitable, for even those interested seldom understand that Zen is but a name for the Absolute and that it must ever remain beyond the grasp of the relative mind. These drag it down to the level of hypothesis and argument; others more foolish still drag it into the gutter as 'beat Zen' and then, perhaps fortunately, throw it aside.

No matter. Zen is beyond destruction, though the present forms in which it is approached will die. So will all other forms of approach, but we in the West must find and use some means to clothe it for a while in terms and forms of effort appropriate to our need.

What follows here is therefore only one attempt, born of personal experience and some forty years of work with others, to suggest but never to lay down a possibly helpful way towards the new awareness. It is a practical course of personal mind-training, which may for some provide an approach to that direct, immediate awareness of Non-duality ('Not One, not Two') which some call Zen. Those who wish to benefit from the course must use it; it is a waste of time to read it, even many times, or to regard it as instruction. And those who use it must develop the will-power to devote themselves to a long period of very hard work. This of course implies some measure of faith that the effort will produce results. I can only say that in many years of using and advocating the course in one form or another I have found that results appear in direct proportion to the amount of work put in. Those who search for marvels, mental or emotional 'kicks' or psychic powers should read no further. What will at first appear will not be comfort, peace of mind or happiness but an increased tension in the mind and a consequent increase of 'suffering'. This I believe to be inevitable, for thus and thus alone we grow.

The course is for those who accept that they are living in a world of relativity, and not in a phantasy of a state of consciousness not yet attained. Buddhism admits an absolute and a relative truth, and in the world of Samsara, the field of the opposites, all knowledge is, from the viewpoint of the Absolute, unreal, illusion. Facing this situation, let us frankly strive for Non-duality with clearly perceived motive; let us train ourselves for a journey, step by step, within the illusion of time. Later, probably much later, when consciousness has been raised to the level of thought illumined by direct vision of Reality, we may with some effect talk in the language of paradox of the futility of effort to achieve anything, or to become what in fact we are, of purposelessness, and of a sudden awareness of supernal Emptiness beyond the reach of time.

But let us not be too clever too soon. We shall in due course truly 'see' that Nirvana is here and now, but not yet; that we are already enlightened, but not yet. Let us be humble, content to begin with what we at present know and seem to be.

The aim of this course, then, is to produce a steady rise in the level of habitual consciousness. When this is achieved I find, from observation and personal experience, that the mind is the more ready for true Zen experience which, though never the *result* of training of any kind, is more likely to arise in minds in a certain condition.

In the course of this training motive will be purified, the self begin to die, and there will appear at first brief 'glimpses' and later more substantial 'moments' of Zen experience, of that Awakening which raised an Indian princeling to the status of Buddha, the All-Enlightened One. On our journey we shall pass through psychic visions and 'hunches' to the plane of brilliant thought, but then, beyond all these, unmistakable, unforgettable, all but incommunicable, to a true 'break-through' to the Absolute. And then if we are wise we shall remember Dr Suzuki's words, that 'Zen is the system of moral discipline built upon the foundation of *satori*'. In other words, the first true break-through is the first step on the path and not the end of it, still less the goal. And with this first experience the need for humility becomes greater than ever before. The Buddhist movement in the West is too full of those who claim, on the strength of a brief experience, 'I am now enlightened', and actually believe it.

It may be reasonably argued that, just as in the Zen story no amount of polishing a tile will turn it into a mirror, so no polishing of the human mind will turn it into the Buddha-mind. True, it need not be emptied; it is already empty. It need not be filled; it is already full. As the Patriach Hui-Neng pointed out, 'the Essence of Mind is intrinsically pure'. But it needs intuition to *see* this to be true. How do we develop the needful faculty?

Again, it may be argued that between the relative and the Absolute there can be no bridge, no possible communication. This is logically true, and Zen training is concerned to break the limitations of such logic. Zen builds the bridge every day by pointing out that none is needed. If the relative and Absolute are truly seen to be one, what need to communicate? If I may collate several extracts from the writings of Dr D. T. Suzuki, 'No causal relationship can be established between Buddhist thought of any form and the actual fact of Satori' [but] 'the main object of the Buddhist life consists in having a certain spiritual revulsion, whereby we are able to leap from the dualistic shore of this individualistic world to the other shore of Nirvana. To effect this revulsion, spiritual discipline is needed, which finally leads up to a certain exalted inner condition [of] enlightenment, self-realization, or the opening of an inner eye'. . . . 'Zen of all the schools of Buddhism, is pre-eminently the religion of enlightenment'.

Let me recapitulate. The wise ones say that there is no point in developing the mind, or seeking to purify or ennoble it, for the mind is already the Buddha-mind, complete, pure and beyond improvement. All that is needed is to observe and know this fact. I repeat, and it is the central theme of this brief volume, HOW? By what process, by what path however steep is such awareness to be achieved? Careful enquiry from those who seem to me to be wise ones, alive or for the moment dead, leads me to believe what one would expect, by a long course of training, varying with the stage of progress of the mind concerned. I have yet to meet a human being to whom this did not apply. There are those, not rare, who have known the meaning of Satori, but that is the beginning, not the end. Then comes the maturing of the experience, and building it into Wisdom/Compassion. Then more experience, deeper, wider for many a life to come.

Meanwhile, most of us are at a low rung of the ladder, and looking for a way of climbing step by step the higher rungs of it. Whatever be one's own experience or progress I believe it to be the duty of every man to make available such steps as he has found upon that way.

BASIC BUDDHISM

I

The Buddha

In an introduction to his translation of the Dhammapada, Dr Radha-krishnan, the Hindu scholar who was for many years President of India, wrote of the Buddha, 'He belongs to the history of the world's thought, to the general inheritance of all cultivated men. Judged by intellectual integrity, moral earnestness and spiritual insight he is undoubtedly one of the greatest figures in history.' H. G. Wells more simply called him the greatest man that ever lived. Some of us dare to call ourselves, with scant humility, his followers, and to use his name. For us he is the man who achieved the Goal completely, who taught the Way to it which he had found and trod.

He is an historic figure, and there is ample evidence that ashes now kept on the high altar of the Maha Bodhi temple in Calcutta came from the body that he used in his final incarnation. He has been given many titles, names and attributes but never that of Creator of the universe nor that of a personal God to be worshipped, who could save a man from the fruits of his folly. He was the latest but not the last of his line, the Fully Awakened One, the All-Enlightened One, the Buddha. Thus we remember him, with gratitude if we accept the value of that virtue, with abounding love and veneration for one whose consciousness became commensurate with the universe, who made it possible for us to become what he became, to live in full awareness of the totality we have not ceased to be.

Gautama Siddhartha was a princeling of the Sakya clan of North-east India. We have much detail of the traditional life to which myth and legend have been added. Of great physical beauty, with a magnificent intellect, he absorbed the wisdom of the sages at his father's court, and by his skill at arms won his bride, Yasodhara. They had a son and were, so far as humans may be, utterly content. But Gautama was heir to a hundred lives of preparation and in this, the last, he was a dedicated man. In time he saw, as each of us must learn to see, old age, disease and death, and the symbol of an ideal beyond worldly happiness. He made the renunciation that we all must make, in small ways to the final stage; he gave up throne and kingdom, home and family, and clothed in rags went off into the jungle, possessed of nothing save an indomitable will to find the cause of the suffering that seemed inherent in the very stuff of life, to eradicate that cause whatever it might be, and to show the Way to such a goal. After long and dire austerities, a summary of those awaiting every man who strives to slay, beyond revival, the last word of self, the meditator, locked in final strife beneath the Bo-Tree at Bodh-Gaya, broke through to Enlightenment. This was no sudden peep of new awareness, no single 'experience' of non-duality but full, complete Awakening to the utmost range of consciousness, deeper and more complete than that of any other man throughout this whole aeon of time. The Buddha knew now what he knew and that it was limitless. The story goes that one Upaka, the heretic, met him and enquired 'Your countenance is serene, your complexion pure and bright. Who is your teacher?'

The Buddha's recorded answer is, I submit, of immense importance to each one of us. 'I have no teacher. I am the All-Enlightened One. I shall go to Benares to set in motion the Wheel of the Law. I shall beat the drum of the Immortal in the darkness of the world.'

That is the claim and Buddhism stands on it. What does it imply? First, that here in the world the Buddha was already in Nirvana. Nirvana is to be won here and now, not in a vague 'beyond'. And secondly, that what a man can do all men can do, for here was a man made perfect and no god. And thirdly, surely, that the Immortal, the Unborn, Uncreate, is achievable by man, is here and now and in the midst of this.

And so he taught, to help all men to train themselves as he had trained himself, deeply to see the Signs of Being which are the triple nature of all things, to seek out and destroy 'the builder of the house of self', to achieve Nirvana in the here and now, for oneself and all mankind. Here was no dogma, no word of revealed authority, no claim of salvation by any Being in or without the universe. In Dr Radhakrishnan's tremendous words, 'He would not let his adherents refuse the burden of spiritual liberty'.

He taught, for some fifty years, all who came to him, kings and Brahmins, warriors and farmers, beggars and criminals. He taught them all according to their need. He founded an Order of his immediate pledged followers. This, the oldest in the world, was never a closed Order. 'Go ye forth', he said to them, 'proclaim the Doctrine glorious, for the benefit of gods and men'. Viharas were founded for the rainy season; for the rest of the year the Bhikkhus' duty was to teach.

Even this prototypical, symbolic life, the ultimate pattern for all of us, came to an end, and the last of his bodies was finally abandoned and burnt. Councils were held to agree the Doctrine. Schools, reflecting the different aspects of the human mind, were formed and spread, South, South-east, East and North and finally in our day West. We have the Teaching, no doubt mangled and degraded by the feebler minds that followed before the least word was written down. And even then, it is obvious that monkish hands have added, subtracted and altered the original text. What is left, however, in seven languages, in a hundred vital volumes, is more than enough teaching for us to digest in a dozen lives to come. We have the Dhamma, or some of it, but let us never forget the Man. Let us love that supreme example of the holy life, with gratitude and the fervent will to follow.

There are, alas, but three Lives of the Buddha in print. Some of us have watched them born and grow. Mrs Adams Beck's *Life of the Buddha*, as it is now called; E. H. Brewster's *Life of the Buddha*, compiled from the Pali Canon, and E. J. Thomas's *The Life of Buddha in Legend and History*; why not read them and study them deeply? Sooner or later we must develop the same tremendous power of will dedicated to the service of mankind, the strength and clarity of intellect, the immeasurable compassion, and the wisdom, expressed with such a gentle sense of humour.

What, then, is the relation of the Buddha, the man, to ourselves? Is it only the memory of a man who lived long years ago? 'Buddhism' itself tells otherwise, and speaks of a large step from history into spiritual experience. This must be taken by every Buddhist, for Buddhism is far more than a mere collection of ideas. We must move from a man to a principle, to the Buddha-principle within. 'Look within', says *The Voice of the Silence*, 'thou art Buddha'. Or, in the comparable rise in Christianity, from Jesus to the Christ-principle, 'I and my Father are one'.

Where is the bridge? Surely in this case via Hinduism. It must never be forgotten that the Buddha and his cultured audience were all Hindus, all versed in the Vedas and the Upanishads of the day. All accepted Brahman as a concept to describe the beyond of the phenomenal world, beyond the triple god-head of Brahmā, Shiva and Vishnu; some went further and spoke of Para-brahman, beyond even that. Remember that Brahmin is a word of praise in the Dhammapada, and never of disparagement. And all these men alike knew that Brahman, or the Unborn, however changing fashion spoke of THAT, is immanent in daily life, and that each and every man already is in a sense Brahman, by virtue of Atman in every mind, the light which is a ray of the ultimate Unborn. To say 'there is no Atman' is surely nonsense, a denial of the spirituality in all that lives. As Dr D. T. Suzuki put it, 'To say there is no Atman, that is not enough. We must go one step farther beyond and say that there is Atman, but this Atman is not on the plane of the relative but on the plane of the Absolute.' (*The Field of Zen*, p. 91.) All this was common ground to the Buddha and his audience, and the Buddha rejected not one word of it.

But about him was a debased Hinduism, and even as Jesus, a Jew, set out to reform Judaism so the Buddha, a Hindu, reformed Hinduism, albeit some five hundred years earlier. He tried to eschew the 'indeterminates', the problems which could never be fully solved nor truly experienced by the intellect alone. These would be understood at a later stage of the Path. Meanwhile, for a long while, let the Buddhist concentrate on the Way, from suffering to the end of suffering, from desire to peace, from what we are to what we would be and truly are, the Atman, a ray of the Light within.

The importance of this mental move, from history to psychology, from the objective to the subjective, from intellectual knowledge to spiritual experience, is profound. Even the famous *Tat twam asi* of Hindu mysticism can remain as the mental proposition that thou, the individual, art THAT, the Ultimate. This can still rest in the field of hypothesis, for debate and allocation to one of the pigeon-holes of thought. But to look within, and to *see*, as a matter of sudden personal experience, that the Buddha-mind, the essence of pure consciousness is here within, within 'myself', yourself and every living thing, this is the 'moment of no time' at which the growing minds begin the long climb to the heart's enlightenment. Without this realization surely the Theravada is mere moral philosophy, with the sole motive of wanting to stop being unhappy. With it, those who hear 'the drum-beat of the Immortal', who seek the Uncreate, who know that 'Self is the lord of self' and glimpse afar the Unborn father of both, these few can receive the Buddha's teaching as the noblest Message ever given to mankind.

The change is from doctrine to experience, and though the breakthrough be sudden the training must be long. From the first brief contact in some life to deeper study in some later life, and finally to the moment when the student emerges from the chrysalis of thought and becomes the dedicated pilgrim on a well-trod Way, thus do we train ourselves.

The change is widely called the moment of conversion, a 'turning about at the seat of consciousness', as it is described in the Mahayana, and though it must be perpetually renewed it is irrevocable. The experience, and all that follows, is a matter of consciousness, and therefore in the field of enlightenment. Its implications are tremendous. First, it is an awareness of all 'things' as parts of one inseverable Whole. It follows that men are brothers, kinsmen of all living things, and there is nothing dead. All forms are forms of the one Life, lit by rays of the one Light. This is now seen as fact and no longer mystical jargon.

But if only the Unborn *is*, and all appearance is, in its seeming separateness, illusion, first it follows that there is no separate self in any man or thing, and *anatta* ('no-self') is perhaps for the first time felt as true. And next, if I am but a felt-to-be separate but in fact unsevered part of one immeasurable Whole, then compassion is in truth the law of life, and it is right to say that Buddhism rests upon the twin pillars of Wisdom and Compassion and that the two are one. We know not Wisdom unless and until it is applied. Compassion is indeed 'the law of laws'; the first step on the Path is truly 'to live to benefit mankind', and even the six glorious virtues a poor second. From self that strives for wisdom to an awareness that there is no separate self to strive and that wisdom, in the world of paradox, is the fruit of its own unceasing application to the all-self of all Life, such is the movement of the heart within. And though the movement will be checked by recurring periods of darkness when the 'I' again takes over, the Light has been seen, and whether one calls this vision mystical, or somehow fits it into the field of scientific knowledge makes no matter. Henceforth the pilgrim is returning, knowingly, to his Father's home.

But a third change flows from awareness of the Buddha-Mind within. We move, henceforth, in terms of learning and teaching in the realm of paradox. Among fellow strivers for the Light of Non-duality— 'not one, not two'—we must understand that we seek and strive for what we already have, that indeed the path, the traveller and the goal are one.

Meanwhile we learn to 'walk on'; here, for there is nowhere else nor ever will be; now, for there will never be but now, and doing this, within the ambit of our karma for the life now being lived. We shall do it each in our own way, using as we will the path of wisdom or devotion or right action, with study and meditation as we find the need, but always striving to apply the wisdom gained for the service of mankind. Such was the Buddha's own example, one which in the lightening darkness of a mind grown stronger we must strive to follow; such is the Buddhist Way.

What did the Buddha teach? In truth we do not know, for no word was written down for at least four hundred years after his passing and the scriptures such as we have them are the product of much editing. But the oldest surviving school, preserving its own canon, is the Theravada, 'the teaching of the Elders', which many regard as the finest moral philosophy extant. Its Three Signs of Being, Four Noble Truths, its doctrine of Karma and Rebirth, Nibbana and the Arhat ideal comprise a message for all that have ears to hear. And the Abhidhamma with its detailed analysis of consciousness provides a field of psychology not yet attained by a Western school today.

But if the Buddha refused to discuss the 'indeterminates' of Self, the First Cause and the like, the Indian mind was fearless in the development of ideas which are but seedlings in the Theravada. Anatta was raised to the final level of Sunyata, the Void; Metta, friendliness, was seen as the divine Compassion which is one with Wisdom, 'the Wisdom that has gone beyond'; and the Bodhisattva ideal was offered as complementary to that of the Arhat. Further still, the Unborn was no longer viewed as the beyond of the born but one with it. Nirvana is here in Samsara, where alone it will be known. We are already what we would be, enlightened but knowing it not, for the darkness of Avidya, ignorance, lies upon our inward-looking eyes.

With the founding of the Ch'an/Zen school one thousand years after the Buddha's passing Buddhism became and has since remained the largest field of human thought. Meta-physics, the prototype of physics, ontology, the science of being, mysticism as an embracing term for viewed awareness of the Unborn; psychology, as the analysis of consciousness with rules for its achievement; ritual, morality, culture and art; here is a field of mind-development with tolerance for all who enter it, unlimited time, from life to life, in which to digest it all, and a steady movement on the Middle Way to a Nirvana which is found to be here and now.

Yet withal the Teaching remains essentially a Way of Life, a road to be trodden and not a body of doctrine for the lecture hall. Let 'Self become the lord of self' as the Dhammapada commands, and this is personal hard work, but as the evolving and enlightened mind perceives the illusion of separation and its own totality, it rises life by life to the moment when it *knows* as the Buddha told mankind he *knew*, that self is ended and Nirvana won.

This was not all. From history to mysticism was a mighty step. But with the concept of the Dharmakaya, with the Adi-Buddha and the Dhyani-Buddhas of Tibet, with the Alaya-Vijnana of the Mind-Only School and above all with Sunyata, the supreme achievement of the 'Wisdom that has gone Beyond', the Buddha-Mind is seen as one with the Essence of all-Mind, the void which yet is full, the nameless Absolute which the Buddha called the 'Unborn, Unoriginated and Unformed'.

Such is Buddha-hood, comparable with Eckhart's Gottheit, 'God-hood', the Parabrahman of the Hindus, the Fana-al-Fana of Persian mysticism. But yet this goal that the Buddha achieved is achievable by all, and when human consciousness is one with the Buddha-mind there is no more to be said, for the Buddha-mind is one with the Unborn. If this is Everest for us it is at present only so with the aid of concept. To *know* it means that belief must be merged in awareness, thought transcended into the field of Prajna-intuition, mere bright words made pale in the full light of enlightenment.

On such a journey the Buddha, renouncing the sweets of Nirvana, became our patient guide. He who knew that Path, each weary, blood-stained foot of it, with self the payment to be made afresh at every stage, remained to speak of it in detail, and Buddhism at its best, or high or low, is a detailed guide-book to that Way. Such is he whom the Master K. H. in a letter to A. P. Sinnett called 'the wisest and the holiest man that ever lived', and we, in the footsteps of unnumbered millions in the last two thousand five hundred years may find this to be true.

But the way that goes up comes down again. The Buddhist does not merely aspire to the heights. His heart is open to the great cry of humanity. Compassion, the 'Law of laws' has made him dedicated to the service of mankind. Whether we move in the vertical path of self-enlightenment which is the Arhat way, or work for the enlightenment of all in the horizontal sweep of pure compassion, in the end we achieve the oneness of Prajna/Karuna, and finding for ourselves the 'Gate-less Gate' to the final path, tread that short but fearful way to its supernal end.

Life after life, as the Buddha taught us, we must train for this adventure, using the law of Karma to remould the mind and human circumstance just so much nearer to the heart's desire. As the cold illusion of separation dies, as the bundle we call character, held in the bondage of desire, is itself dissolved, so the mystery of consciousness within the Unconscious is slowly, excitingly attained. Each thing, here and now, is seen to be as divine as anything is or will be; each part *is* the Whole. The form about *is* the Emptiness of all things and the very

Emptiness *is* form. These foolish opposites grow tiresome and untrue. The gradual path to sudden enlightenment is at our feet; we are that path and with every breath we are slowly treading it.

In brief, as Huang Po pointed out, 'All the Buddhas and all sentient beings are nothing but the One Mind, beside which nothing exists'. It is our role and total duty to find this to be true.

2

Four Noble Truths

The Four Noble Truths are central to Buddhism, and if true are true to all men, without reference to time or place. In briefest form they state that life is inseparable from suffering (*dukkha*) in one form or another; that its basic cause is selfish desire, the craving of the ego-self for its own satisfaction; that the cause can be removed by any man, and removed by the system of physical, moral and spiritual training known as the Noble Eightfold Path.

That the teaching is central to Buddhism is clear from repeated words in the Pali Canon of the Theravada School, and it seems to be equally central in all other schools of Buddhism. 'One thing I teach, O Bhikkhus, sorrow and the end of sorrow', said the Buddha. And again: 'It is through not understanding these Four Noble Truths that we have wandered so long around this cycle of rebirth, you and I'.

The word *dukkha*, however, is of very wide range, and covers, as set out in the Scriptures, 'birth, decay, sickness and death; to be joined to the unloved or separated from the loved', and failure to achieve one's desires. But it means much more than this. Frustration, competition, the emotions of fear and hate, the imperfection of the mind-machine and its ignorance, the failure to achieve ideals; all this is suffering. And, for the compassionate heart, the sufferings of all others even when one's own are minimal.

It is one of the Three Signs of Being pointed out by the Enlightened One as facts which all can verify. That all is changing all the time is, to most of us, a fact beyond dispute. That to this fact or law there are no exceptions is not so obvious but of profound importance. For the self, each and every form of it, is here included. There is in man no permanent, abiding principle or soul or self which is immortal and unchanging. To the extent that there is in every man a spark of the Divine or Absolute which Buddha called the 'Unborn, Unoriginated, Unformed', this principle or Atman is not his alone. All that is his, for the duration of one life on earth, is changing all the time. But he will not have it so. He claims for 'himself' whatever his desire can gain. It changes and decays and dies, he with it. In the result he suffers.

Of all the religions of the world Buddhism alone makes suffering central and explains the cause of it; not some extra-cosmic God, nor fate, nor Destiny by any name, but himself, his own blind silly self.

Yet some of the suffering that all endure is not our personal or even collective 'fault'. It is inherent in the nature of things and will endure for the life of the manifested universe. The Unborn first appears to our eyes as One, which divides, for reasons immaterial here, into Two and thence, for two alone is inconceivable, into Three which is the basic trinity of manifestation. But it is as Two that we feel its devastating force, for we stand as the median third between the polar opposites of positive/negative, spirit/matter, good and evil, and are torn by the tension which at one and the same time binds all opposites together and tears them apart. Meanwhile we choose, as choose we must, and with every choice the 'other' is enemy. In duality we cannot be complete, and the awareness of unending incompleteness is itself a form of suffering.

Already filled with the sense of strain, of insufficiency, frustration, general 'want', man adds to his own misery and that of all mankind. In his ignorance he fights for his own side against the other, male versus female, East versus West, the million parts against the many-seeming whole; and this unending war within is 'projected', to use the modern term, on to all about him, appearing between races, groups and nations as perennial war. It is an unpalatable truth that so long as the war in every mind continues, so long will the mass projection known as war be the visible result. We watch ambition, aggression, competition between factions, parties, religions, nations, man and man, and with all there is the same phrase used, the fight for survival.

In such perpetual war, with a rising population to provide the 'cannon fodder' for the lords of power, what chance is there for beauty, quietude and peace? All is destroyed and polluted in the rising clamour of angry sound. And while the intellect is worshipped and the heart is starved, all this takes place in the name of Progress!

This is fact, and therefore not to be condemned as pessimism. This is seeing, seeing things as they are. Of course there is and will be happiness, but what is happiness, when honestly examined, worth? It is always temporary, always to some extent 'self'ish, always attached to the circumstances which provide the happiness and these, like all else, will at any moment change and be no more.

What, then, is the cause of all this 'misery, lamentation and despair'?

In the classic words of the Pali Canon 'It is that craving which gives rise to fresh rebirth, and bound up with lust and greed finds, now here now there, ever fresh delight . . .'. This craving includes attachment to the objects of sense ('having a good time') and worse, sensuality (*kama*) which involves the imprisonment of consciousness in what is at best animal enjoyment.

A common translation of the Sanskrit *trshna*, Pali *tanha*, is desire, but the use of this English term has led to grave misunderstanding. For desire is neither good nor evil. By desire was the Unborn born into Samsara; by desire THAT 'breathed out', and by it the many strive to return. Desire produced what the Buddha called 'the unrolling and rolling up of the worlds' and by its force, or not at all, the aspiring pilgrim will attain Nirvana.

What, then, has gone wrong? It is the use of the desire, its direction, purpose, aim. For desire itself is essentially creative; it creates all forms with what Sri Krishna Prem has called its 'bursting quality', a bursting out into ever new forms, whether the cosmic pressure to create new universes, or yours and mine to produce some new idea. 'Behind will stands desire', as the Eastern saying has it. If will is the motive force, as the engine in the car, it is desire, the driver, who decides where it will go. Raised, it will lead to Nirvana; debased, drawn down and held by *kama*, sensuous, lustful craving for self, it fetters the higher principles of mind and binds the would-be Buddha yet more firmly to the Wheel.

According to the late Dr D. T. Suzuki, desire, rightly directed, leads to compassion. 'Desire', he says in *Mysticism, Christian and Buddhist* (pp. 73 and 127), is not to be understood negatively. 'The Buddhist training consists in transforming *trshna* into *karuna*, ego-centred love into something universal. . . . When Buddhists let *trshna* work in its own way without being impeded by anything else, *trshna*, "thirst" or "craving", comes to be known as *mahakaruna*, absolute compassion.' It is surely foolish, then, to attempt to crush it out or to escape from it.

The cause of suffering, perhaps, is better seen as low, unworthy craving in the interest of 'self', which for the Western mind may be an easier concept to understand. What, then, is self as a cause of suffering? First, it must not be confused with the personality. This is the mask or outward seeming of the man, within which the mind exists in long-enduring tension, dragged down hourly by the claims of self, and yearning all the while to rise to its own inherent being, in Mind-Only, the Buddha-Mind.

It is not easy to collate the personality as understood in Western psychology with the five *skandhas* of the Pali Canon, but the difficulty need not trouble us here. What matters is the level reached by the higher ranges of consciousness and the control which they can exercise upon the collective mask or personality. The latter is not to be despised. Man's lower 'vehicles', or bases of consciousness, have evolved in their own way from the deeps of 'matter', and we now each live with our collection of higher qualities or vehicles in an animal with animal needs and desires. Truly, 'Self must be Lord of self; what other Lord should there be'? as the Dhammapada has it. But it is surely right that the personality, entirely new in each rebirth, should have in a sense its own ambitions within the ambit of the commonweal. In his reasonable desire to be a success in life a young man will inevitably seem 'selfish' to more developed minds, but a normal youth of either East or West is not concerned with the salvation of mankind but rather with 'getting on in life', with being a success in his chosen career. Is he to be blamed for such ambition?

But somewhere this process of growth to maturity goes wrong. Some part of the personality becomes anti-social and evil, and develops a craving which leads to suffering in this life and in lives to come. The cause would seem to be basically Avidya, ignorance, 'not-seeing' and in particular what in the *Tathagata-guhya Sutra* is referred to as 'the heresy of individual existence'. The evil of this heresy is shown by the words added in the description of it given in *The Voice of the Silence* which, translated, reads 'the great heresy of separateness, which weans thee from the rest'. Here's the rub. The false belief is bad enough, for it breeds a sense of difference and hence arrogant self-importance; but in weaning one from the rest it moves into a field of near-insanity, the belief that others are unimportant save as they serve or hinder the needs of this particular self. Here is the ultimate blasphemy, that this bundle of attributes, with a name and address and job, is totally and eternally different from all other forms of the Unborn in the manifested universe.

For there *are* no others; there *is* no difference. The whole of Samsara and all that therein is, reveals but the Absolute incarnate. Samsara in the eyes of the Absolute is *maya*, illusion; so is the Absolute in the eyes of those within Samsara. Both are true; untrue. Of both we can but say 'Not-One, not-Two'.

Once this is intuitively understood, the unceasing tension of life is seen for what it is, metaphysical and quite impersonal; and the individual is seen as a unit of life with its own 'conditioning', its present *dharma* or duty to perform, and its immediate purpose, to play out its part—'Not my will but Thine be done'—within the supernal purpose of the ultimate Unborn.

But such a viewpoint, such dedication to the pursuit of Enlightenment is seldom for the young. They have their primal energy to harness and exhaust in the futilities of daily life. Only later will an inward hunger for something more be evident, and lead to that 'turning about at the seat of consciousness' which is true conversion.

What, then, of the ego, in the Western sense, of the undesirable shadow-self, the self that has gone wrong, a dustbin full of elements of thought and character which we, the higher qualities of Mind, deplore?

In the first place, as already indicated, it is not to be confused with the personality, which in terms of growth is normal. The ego is abnormal, however common among men, and fruitful of unending suffering. The man 'with a chip on his shoulder', with endless feelings easily hurt, is a social nuisance at all periods of human history. Thwarted in his personal ambition, his aggressive behaviour rises to conceal the inward-rising fear of insufficiency. Its folly feeds upon itself, and with the least success, however brutally won in the face of others' rights and needs, it swells to horrible and finally insane proportions.

But it is no part of the legitimate make-up of that form of life in the universe known as man. I see it rather as an abnormal growth of living tissue which, if not too large may be reduced, as doctors would say, and reabsorbed into the body, but which usually calls for the knife. A better analogy is cancer, for it is of the essence of cancerous growth that the life-force has lost its way, and once out of control can destroy the body corporate.

The self or ego is not, however, a thing to be deplored or attacked, still less to be repressed or concealed. It is just a very foolish idea, fed by aberrant aspects of the personality to monstrous size; but with the whole flow of the life-force, newly dedicated to impersonal ends, there is nothing to spare for the fatuous balloon of ego.

The Third Noble Truth is a matter of logic, that to remove the condition we remove the cause. But if the root-cause is the ego-self, with its misdirected desire born of illusion, can one let go of it, drop it, starve it of life? Yes, but further facts must be faced, one of them that there are at least two selves to be considered, whatever the Theravadins say today. For even the Pali Canon is filled with references to the higher and lower aspects of self, the higher, which Hinduism and Mahayana Buddhism know as the Atman, and the lower, which the higher must either drop, disentangle itself from, or best of all see to

C

be complete illusion. The problem, in brief, is not what ought to be done but how to do it. *How* do 'I' let go of 'me'?

If the above analysis be right, it is the aberrant aspect of the total man, the part that has gone off the rails into the heresy of separateness, that must be squarely faced and, as a false belief, destroyed. How shall we bring the consciousness of total man to the new awareness that life is one and indivisible, that 'all distinctions are falsely imagined', that when the Buddha-Mind is rediscovered 'there *are* no *others*'?

One can cope with the ego-self in either of two ways, in the alternative or by an exercise in seeing the two as one. To deflate the self by reasoning, clear seeing and meditation, or by raising consciousness to expand awareness (not *our* awareness) of the growing Self towards its parent, Buddha-Mind, until no energy is left to inflate the ego. ('Forgoing self the universe grows I.') But whether there be no self or nothing else but SELF is a matter of words or point of view—the result is the same; 'the builder of the house is seen, its rafters broken and the ridge-pole destroyed. Never more shall this woe-producing foolishness trouble us again.'

This is the Middle Way between the opposites of self. As Dr Suzuki has written, 'Enlightenment consists in seeing into the meaning of life as the interplay of the relative ego with the absolute ego. In other words, it is seeing the absolute ego as reflected in the relative ego and acting through it'. When the self has subsided the Buddha-Mind can flow through all its vehicles from high to low, in pure alignment of the transmission of energy, the perfect machine, in modern terms, for the expression of force. But, one final word, the awareness achieved by this Zen seeing is not our awareness. In the now famous phrase of the late Father Merton in his *Mystics and Zen Masters*, 'Zen insight is not our awareness, but Being's awareness of itself in us'.

To return to suffering. We have examined it, accepted it and seen its cause. By lifting the heart and mind we shall rise above it, by refusing to react to it *as pain*. As we read in *On Trust in the Heart*,

Do not try to drive pain away by pretending that it is not real;
Pain, if you seek serenity in oneness, will vanish of its own accord.

What, then, is the Way that leads to the end of suffering? As our friend Professor Abe of Japan has recently written, 'Buddhism teaches how to become a Buddha'. It is not a mere set of doctrines, but a Way of spiritual self-development leading to the full Enlightenment achieved by Gautama the Buddha, and achievable in time by all. It is thus first and last a way of action, and all scholarship 'about it and about' leads no one by that effort nearer to the Goal.

Its purpose is, at the lowest, to remove the cause of suffering; at its highest, to achieve Enlightenment. In the Buddhist Scriptures we read of it at three levels; that of the Pali Canon which provides a magnificent system of moral training and mind development up to a certain stage; that of the Mahayana ideal of the Bodhisattva and his six *paramita* virtues, all of which are aspects of the last, Prajna, ultimate Wisdom; and the highest of all, which reads as nonsense in plain English, of No-Views, No-Purpose, up to No-Mind or Buddha-Mind in which the path, the pilgrim and the goal are one. Then only is each step trodden as utterly 'right', for all that is done is 'an infinite way of doing finite things'.

It is possible, I think, to extract from the world's religious literature a clear distinction between the individual's own way through the darkness of Avidya, Ignorance ('the ways to the One are as many as the lives of men'), and the entrance to the final, or 'short' path, as the Tibetans call it, beyond which 'There is no going back. Behind me stands a closèd door'. Beyond this entrance, 'the Gateless Gate' of Zen Buddhism, the pupil will be guided, for 'when the pupil is ready the Master appears'. Until then each one of us must blunder and bump our way in the darkness, climbing three feet, perhaps, only to slip back two. No matter; the Road has two rules only: Begin and Continue, and the Buddha left us a detailed guide-book for the Way.

But it must be trodden, every weary step of it. There is no by-pass nor ever will be, and no short cuts whatever. We tread it on our own two feet, alone, yet feeling in the darkness a million more ahead of us, beside us and behind. There is no chance nor luck nor fortune, good or bad, upon the Way; each moment, each event, is the net result of a million causes each of our own fathering. Yet because we are interdependent and interrelated as the children of one Father, the One Life-force which is the 'Unborn' in manifestation, we help and hinder each other in all our thoughts and actions to the very threshold of Nirvana.

It is a Path to the end of suffering, but along its length we shall suffer rather more than less, for the Way is a process of self-suicide, and the self, the unreal thought-creation of our folly, is most unwilling to die! Hence tension rising in a mind forever torn between the claims of self and the aspirations born of a new vision of Reality.

For a while there will be merit acquired, and we shall hear of a tradition of merit transferred, but the growing mind will seek no

35

reward for deeds well done or service rendered. Indeed, in time there will remain no self to whom credit could be entered up. The Path is one of perpetual loss, the progressive losing of possessions visible and invisible, of prestige and the desire for it. As a Bhikkhu has recently written, 'the Buddhist way of life starts with renunciation', but this reminds one of the saying in Talbot Mundy's *Om*, 'There is no such thing as sacrifice; there is only opportunity to serve'.

Why do we tread the Path, or try to? What is our purpose and motive?—they are not the same. Are we concerned with self-improvement or self-suicide, with the salvation of myself or the salvation of mankind? It is written in the *Tao Te Ching*, 'the sage has no self; he makes the self of the people his self'. Or, as Dr D. T. Suzuki put it, 'Buddhists have almost nothing to do with Buddha, but with their fellow beings'. But Eckhart, surely one of the greatest men the West has produced, put it at its highest. 'If a person were in such a rapturous state as St Paul once entered, and he knew of a sick man who wanted a cup of soup, it would be far better to withdraw from the rapture for love's sake, and serve him who is in need.'

And motive is paramount. As the master K. H. wrote to A. P. Sinnett of the conditions of chelaship in his Tibetan school, 'We judge men by their motives and the moral effect of their actions; for the world's false standards and prejudice we have no respect'.

As an African sage said to an English visitor, speaking of his own traditional version of this ancient Path, 'the length of the road is only the length of the step', and there is plenty of time, itself an illusion, for this timeless journey. According to the clear teaching of the Pali Canon of the Southern School of Buddhism, and the general tradition of Buddhism in all its schools, the process of rebirth, or as the Bhikkhu Rahula calls it, re-existence, on the analogy of work/sleep, work/sleep, and work again, applies to all humanity. The word used to describe the changing, growing bundle of characteristics which moves from life to life is immaterial. I prefer the word character, but it is the process which is important for our purposes. As a Japanese Zen Roshi put it, 'Should your yearning be too weak to lead you to emancipation in your present lifetime you will undoubtedly gain Self-realization in the next; just as yesterday's work half done was finished easily today'.

What is this Self, whom the master Rinzai, founder of the Rinzai school of Zen, called 'the true man of no rank'? Dr Suzuki called it 'a kind of metaphysical self in opposition to the psychological or ethical self which belongs to the finite world of relativity', and, 'enlightenment', he says, in a phrase already quoted, 'is seeing the absolute ego reflected in the relative ego and acting through it'. Which in turn is echoed by Father Thomas Merton: 'Zen insight is not our awareness, but Being's awareness of itself in us'. 'Being' here would be called in Buddhism the Buddha-Mind, or 'the Unborn, Unoriginated, Unformed' as it is described in the Pali Canon. If there is still confusion over the Theravadin statement, quite unsupported in their canon, that there is no self of any kind, is not Dr Suzuki obviously right in saying that 'the denial of Atman maintained by the earlier Buddhists refers to Atman as the relative ego and not the absolute ego, the ego after enlightened experience'?

Such is the pilgrim treading the long way to the entrance to the final Path, the almost perpendicular climb to the top of Everest. The treading needs no apparatus in our daily life—no shrine or rosary, no ritual of prayer or praise. Its steps are eight, but this is pure convention, and in a sense we tread all eight of them at once. The Pali terms are difficult to render by any single word in English, but the sense is here with 'Right', Right Views, Right Motive, Right Speech, Right Action, Right Livelihood, Right Effort, Right Mindfulness and Right Samadhi, a high state of concentration which is, however, short of enlightenment.

1. *Right Views*. There are many versions of these, the Pali Canon favouring just the Four Noble Truths. Hui-Neng, however, says that 'Right Views are transcendent, wrong are worldly', and he adds, 'Erroneous views keep us in defilement while right views remove us'. This reflects the Zen insistence on 'right seeing', seeing things as they are (*tathata*), or 'in their own being' (*swabhava*), which needs the eye of Prajna to be wakened, the Wisdom 'by which Buddha sees all things in their proper order, as they should be', as Dr Suzuki puts it. No wonder that some say Right Views should be at the end of the Path rather than the beginning!

2. *Right Mindedness*. This covers motive, the right reason for beginning to tread the Path, and right motive is, as already shown, of paramount importance.

3, 4 *and* 5 are concerned with Sila, morality, or as I prefer to call it, character-building, the true foundation of the Buddhist way of life, on which all study, meditation and the development of powers should be securely based. Without at least some tramlines of right conduct, some internal self-imposed discipline, the strongest mind may fail. 'Self must be lord of self; what other lord should there be?', as the Dhammapada rightly points out, and the Path should be trodden

37

from the first with a mind awakening to Wisdom and a heart to Compassion, for the two are one. The Bodhisattva mind, with its myriad 'skilful means' for doing good soon learns to distinguish good from evil, though no definition will cover each occasion. A working rule can be that all that moves to the One, to unity, to wholeness, is at our stage of evolution good, and all that tends to diversity and separation, or springs from this belief is, comparatively, wrong and evil. This seems echoed by Arnold Price who, in his translation of the Diamond Sutra profoundly suggests that 'evil is negative, and merely exists in so far as Reality is seen from the point of view of diverse particularity'.

But while the brain argues the heart knows, and the truth is simple. There was a jingle quoted largely when I was a child, written by Ella Wheeler Wilcox.

> Do the work that's nearest, though it's dull at whiles,
> Helping when you meet them lame dogs over stiles.

The quality of the verse is humble but the sentiment is surely worthy of the Dhammapada. And if we do right the mind is by the act ennobled; if wrong, we suffer, and learn our error from the just hand of Karma. Truly we are punished by our sins, not for them.

The key to choosing between right and wrong seems to be non-attachment, for such action does not bind. Indeed, it has been said that no action binds us, only our attitude to it, the amount of self involved. The perfect act is difficult indeed, involving as it does right motive, means, time and place, and indifference to the result, and it is soon forgotten. It must be done now, for there is no other time. Who said, 'Only sages and children live utterly in the present'? He must have been a sage.

Can we learn to 'live life as life lives itself', without fuss, seeing all things to be rightly what they are, and prepared to leave them so without our interference? If so, we can allow ourselves to be utterly occupied with the job in hand. If this be our habit we may see the truth in the curious teaching in the Tao Te Ching, 'the Sage never attempts great things, and thus he can achieve what is great'. Whatever the size of the enterprise, we can only take the next step on the way to its fulfilment. The result of our action will not be perfect but then, as R. H. Blyth says somewhere, 'Perfection means, not perfect actions in a perfect world, but appropriate action in an imperfect one'.

Thus the school of right action is daily life. 'Those who wish to train themselves (spiritually) may do so at home. It is quite unnecessary for them to stay in monasteries.' And this from Hui-Neng, the founder of the school of Zen Buddhism!

The same applies to Right Speech and Right Livelihood. The former is more important than generally recognized, for sound creates on every plane, for good or ill. It is not easy to control. As St James found out, man has tamed most things but 'the tongue can no man tame'. The ideal that every word spoken should be both true and helpful is too much for most of us, but its value on the Way is obvious. Right Livelihood should be compatible with the Buddhist views on morality. It is a high ideal for the Western Buddhist, and we honour the men who, finding their work quite incompatible with their Buddhist ideals, just drop the job, at whatever sacrifice to self and home. How lovely to have earned the right to spend one's days in a job that is total service to those about one.

There comes a time on the Path when some power from the deeps within takes over, at least in moments of great stress. It is impersonal, as though a living and intelligent Law. In the speech which made him famous, Emerson spoke of these laws 'which execute themselves. They are out of time, out of space and not subject to circumstance'. Edwin Arnold called it 'a Power divine which moves to good; only its laws endure', but it has no name. Call it the Voice of the Silence, the will of God or the strong arm of the Unborn, it matters not. It is, and if we get out of the way it is omnipotent. There remains but what the master Takuan called 'the unfoldment of doing', a quiet, ceaseless 'walking on'. For the Path is trodden by the whole man, the best and the worst of him, the eyes of the Spirit and the muddy boots withal. When such a man acts out each situation, 'leaving no trace' as the Zen men say, he sets an example, and such is in the end the ultimate form of teaching. For the Buddha's power lay in what he was—proof that the Path existed and could be trodden by all men to the same supernal end. As a later Master advised his followers, 'Let your light so shine before men that they may see your good works and glorify your Father which is in Heaven' or, as the Buddhist would say, show proof of the Buddha-Mind within. As L. H. Myers in *The Root and the Flower* made a wise old teacher say, 'No man can more greatly benefit his fellows than by the force of his example, the spectacle of his achieved holiness', for this holiness is the outward seeming of the Light within, the light of enlightenment.

6. *Right Effort* is what a member here called 'getting up a head of steam' for the final stages, and the steam is needed, every pound of it.

7 *and* 8. On Mindfulness, and Concentration and Meditation much has been written, and there is a chapter on the subject later herein. Suffice it here to say that before we can use an instrument, for good or ill, we must learn to control it. We must be able to concentrate at will before we can use this ability in the new and exciting field of meditation. And before we begin to meditate we should know why, for self or something nobler. Methods are countless yet much the same, and all may lead, in time, to some experience of the beyond of all duality, of the Absolute which the Buddha called the Unborn, and when achieved in depth this new awareness is, as all agree, unmistakable, incommunicable but unforgettable.

And it all takes place in the mind, the journey, the pilgrim and the goal. 'I am the Way, the Truth and the Life', said Jesus, for nothing *is* save the Buddha-Mind. And the Goal? Silence, and a finger pointing the Way.

Pleasure-Pain

Blue sunlight, soft on sleepy eyes.
A terrace of content, from duty free.
Below, as each day lives and dies,
The murmur of the sapphire sea.

Of such is pleasure, the heart's quietude,
And every sense released from memory,
Replete with each its own beatitude.

And this is pain, the riven heart at feud
With all endeavour; duties yet undone;
Uncompassed vision under clouded skies,
The burden of awareness yet unwon.

Is each illusion, each but a severed twin?
It must be that on earth, here, now, in this
The lion-heart shall sudden enter in
And find no difference.
                O rootless bliss,
To dwell within a sun-illumined mind
Beyond the sad delights of human kind!

3

Buddhism Teaches Rebirth

Fashions change, in doctrine as all else, and Western Buddhism is no exception. Forty years ago Karma and Rebirth were all but sufficient; then the Eightfold Path gained prominence, and Buddhist ethics. After the war the Nidanas were claimed as the cure-all for our ignorance, and then Meditation swept aside all doctrine in favour of just sitting, and hoping for the best. This, of course, is exaggeration but it shows a tendency.

There has been a complementary attack on doctrines at the time unpopular, and a few years ago the doctrine of Karma, universal in the Orient, was suddenly scorned on the ground that no one cause could possibly produce a single effect, or progress would be impossible. But no Buddhist ever suggested that one cause produced one effect. The actual doctrine, in its shortest and most pungent form is, 'That being so, this arises; this ceasing to be, that ceases to be.' A million causes go to produce 'that'; together, they being so, 'this' arises. But 'this' arising, a million other situations and people will be in some way affected.

This is cosmic law, the harmony of the universe which, being broken, calls for adjustment. But if such is the law, the effect must surely return to the cause of which it is an inseverable part, and therefore to the causer. In simple language, the man who offended pays. Is the man who pays the same or not the same as he who incurred the debt? And at the body's death, with a load of unpaid causes in his mind, who pays, and when, and where? Surely the doctrine of Rebirth, as plainly stated a hundred times in the Pali Canon, is a necessary corollary of Karma? Why, then, is it suddenly laid aside and, by a number of persons calling themselves Buddhists, clearly not believed?

I do not know, but I hold that it is important to enquire. For I personally believe that the teaching of the Buddhist Scriptures is true, and I have the greater part of mankind on my side. Indeed, I entirely accept the Bhagavad Gita, in the charming translation of Sir Edwin Arnold,

> 'Tis but as when one layeth
> His worn out robes away,
> And taking new ones, sayeth
> 'These will I wear today!'
> So putteth by the Spirit
> Lightly its garb of flesh,
> And passeth to inherit
> A residence afresh. . . .

I regard this as excellent Buddhism. And Matthew Arnold explains its purpose:

> We shall unwillingly return
> Back to this meadow of calamity,
> This uncongenial place, this human life;
> And in our individual human state
> Go through the sad probation all again,
> To see if we will poise our life at last,
> To see if we will now at last be true
> To our own only true deep-buried selves
> Being one with which we are one with the whole world. . . .

This is indeed life's purpose and our goal. As Polonius puts it to Laertes,

> This above all: to thine own self be true,
> And it must follow, as the night the day,
> Thou canst not then be false to any man.

But quotation from the poets can be endless, for the poets know. In prose and verse one may gather a volume of belief in Karma and some form of Rebirth, and there are indeed two volumes for our bookshelves in the last few years.[1]

Is there support for belief in Rebirth? One wonders where to begin. Of proof, to a doubting mind there can be none, for what in the spiritual field has ever yet been proved? Yet reason and analogy speak for it. If Nature's rhythm is work and rest, work and rest, in day and night;

[1] *Reincarnation.* Head and Cranston. Julian Press, New York, 1961.
Reincarnation in World Thought. Head and Cranston. Julian Press, New York, 1967.
See also: *Karma and Rebirth.* Christmas Humphreys. Murray, 1943.

if the garden shows the cycle of birth, growth, decay and death, and then rebirth, must man be the exception? But this is not 'authority', and there are those who, in the face of the Kalama Sutta, look for authority even in the mouth of Buddhism. They will find it in quantity if they take the trouble to look. The Buddha as a Hindu would have absorbed the law of Karma/Rebirth with his mother's milk, and where does he ever deny it? The Buddhist Goal is itself described as 'release from rebirth', from attachment to the ever-rolling Wheel of Rebirth to which desire, so long as it is in the least 'self'ish, binds us. And in due course the Wayfarer, as Mrs Rhys Davids calls him, 'enters the stream', and thereafter is soon a 'once-returner', that is, having but one more birth before achieving the state of consciousness when personal desire is dead.

Are all our previous births forgotten? They are not. Not only does the Buddha speak in the greatest detail of his past lives but the disciple is trained to remember his own. Many of us do, and in far more detail than we remember periods but thirty or forty years removed in time. And analysts have taken patients back to memories of the womb, and further back, to memories of the death that preceded birth.

Why this resistance, then, to a doctrine that alone explains so much that nothing else explains? The 'accidents' of class, and sex, of colour and environment; of mental make-up, introvert or extravert; of early likes and dislikes, aptitudes and inabilities. *Are* these accidents, attributable to the twin dummies of heredity and environment? Are we what we are because of our birth and education, or were we guided to the family and circumstance in which we received our present 'name and form' by the magnetic affinity of past causation? Are infant prodigies yet explained, save by the doctrine of rebirth? Is many an illness karmic born, the slow development of causes long ago produced and now at last maturing?

There must be reasons for the present lowered interest in one of the oldest doctrines of mankind. I know of several. Some students say, 'I do not like it. I do not *want* to be reborn'. Nor, when hit on the head by a very large hail-stone, do *I* approve of the law of gravity, but I do not disbelieve it. Others complain that they do not know how it works. Nor do I understand electricity, but I use an electric razor happily. There are those who announce that all these rebirth stories pertain but to mythology. But mythology is now accepted as the shrine of racial truth. 'It is the last ditch of the ego', I hear a number say. So it is, and it will take many lives before that tiresome illusion is destroyed. There is a modern school of compromise. Rebirth, they say, occurs each moment of time; it is instantaneous on the arising of the previous set of circumstances. This is classic Buddhism, but it does not follow, as they claim, that man is *nothing but* a concatenation of karmic impulse, each new 'person' arising and disappearing with every breath. What happens to this karmic impulse at the last breath of that complex entity? I say, with the Buddhist Scriptures, that it rests, before returning for another million 'moments' on the Way.

But all these are but quibbles compared with a further two objections. The first is that rebirth makes escape impossible, and the vast majority of mankind is forever trying to escape from the consequence of its foolish causes. But the very Scriptures say that this is impossible. 'Not in the sky nor in the sea, nor in a cave in the mountains can a man escape from his evil deeds', says the Dhammapada; nor at the body's death. He will be brought back by his own desire and made to face them.

Yet the real objection, strangely enough, is old and fundamental. It is the clash between this doctrine, which the Buddha clearly taught, and another, which he also taught but which from an early age was, I believe, misunderstood and tragically degraded. As J. G. Jennings put it in *The Vedantic Buddhism of the Buddha*:

'The Buddha accepted so much of the doctrine of transmigration as declares the endless results of all actions of the individual, but the theory of personal reward and punishment in successive lives is radically inconsistent with his characteristic doctrine of No Self, or the impermanence of individuality (*sabbe dhamma an-atta*), and with altruism, being in essence individualistic.'

In other words, as rebirth clashes with the negative, monkish doctrine of Anatta, not any self at all, then it, together with compassion, must go! For what, if there be no self at all, remains at death to be reborn?

So it all comes back to An-atta, the untrue self which builds the house of illusion. 'Now have I found you,' proclaimed the Buddha on achieving full enlightenment. 'Never again shall you build this house (of self)....' But note the preceding verse of the Dhammapada, in which this famous passage appears. 'Through many weary rounds of rebirth have I sought the builder of this house....' It was a long search for the Buddha, as it will be for us, of lives, not moments!

What did the Buddha teach on self? He was brought up as a Hindu and knew the Indian teaching on the Self (Atman) of man as one with the param-Atman of the universe. 'When Gotama began his mission by advising men to seek thoroughly for the Atma, and ended by bidding men live as having Atma for their lamp and refuge, he spoke within the atmosphere of current religious Immanence, using its phraseology.' Thus Mrs Rhys Davids,[1] in her day the leading Pali scholar in the West. She therefore begins her list of 'ten things which Gotama the Buddha will *not* have taught' with: 'that the man, the very man: self, spirit, soul, purusa is not real'. For her, a life student of Theravada Buddhism, the Buddha's concern was with a Wayfarer upon a Way. 'How to Wayfare from this to That: here was life's problem.' And this was a long journey. But Mrs Rhys Davids goes farther still. In her *Indian Religion and Survival* she writes that 'early Buddhism gave India a more definite doctrine, cult or theory of rebirth than any other religion before or since'.

In the Pali Canon the Buddha refused to support or deny a Self, partly because he wished to avoid inclusion in any of the rival schools of the day, and partly because such argument 'did not conduce to peace of mind, Nirvana'. He wanted his disciples to concentrate on the long way through the lives in which, by perpetual self-training, they would remove the Fetters, eliminate the Stains, let the Three Fires die for want of fuelling and so be free of Illusion.

If the Buddha, then, taught Atta, as his brilliant predecessors in the field of Indian thought, what did he say was Not-self, An-atta? He is quite specific. It is the five skandhas, the constituents of personality in which there is no permanent Self to be found. The rest is silence, for of the 'Unborn', of which the Atta is but a reflection, nothing helpful may be said.

Are there, then, two types of self in the Pali Canon? Miss I. B. Horner, a pupil of Mrs Rhys Davids and the present President of the Pali Text Society, shows that this is so. In a famous article reprinted in *The Middle Way* (Vol. 27 p. 76) she lists some seventeen passages from the Pali Canon which make this clear. The 'lesser self' and the 'greater self' are clearly distinguished, and the 'great self' is described as 'a dweller in the immeasurable'. But the Dhammapada, the most famous text in the Canon, will itself suffice. 'Self is the lord of self. What other lord could there be?' And again, 'Self is the lord of self, and self self's bourne', i.e. the very goal of all endeavour. If it is possible to lift the Buddhist teaching nearer still to the Hindu original, look at 'The Self in thee (I claim a capital here) knows what is true and what is false'. Every mystic since the world began would agree.

Let us look again at the doctrine of An-atta *as the Buddha taught it.* It is that there is no unchanging entity or principle in *any or all of the skandhas. As so stated* there is here no conflict with the doctrine of

[1] 'Things he will not have taught', From *A Volume of Indian and Iranian Studies* presented to Sir E. Denison Ross. 1940.

rebirth. But the monks would not leave this statement alone. Attacking the concept of the Atman as degraded in the Buddha's day to a thing, the size of a thumb, in the human heart, they swung too far. 'No self, no self' they cried, and in time produced the joyless, cramping doctrine as drearily proclaimed today. I prefer to agree with Mrs Rhys Davids that the Buddha was concerned with a Way and a Wayfarer, who is urged to train himself, to be ever 'mindful and self-possessed', to 'strive mightily'—as were the Buddha's dying words. Such men move to the More until released from attachment to the Wheel of Rebirth in conscious awareness of the Unchanging.

This will take time, far more than one life allowed by Christian doctrine. The Buddha spoke, with his vision supporting the teaching of his gurus, of the 'evolution and involution of aeons' which, in the esoteric tradition of the East, as outlined in *The Secret Doctrine* of H. P. Blavatsky, is called the breathing out and the breathing in of Parabrahman, the Absolute, which the Buddha called the 'Unborn'. Only rebirth can allow the evolving Self/Not-self to grow from Avidya to Prajna, from the fact of the Buddha within to its full awareness, along a Way which Mrs Davids calls the 'Between' of 'thou art That'.

What, then, is reborn? I submit the following suggestions. And first, that it does not greatly matter to us, now, here, engaged in the next step on the Way. If told that it is a 'discrete continuum of karmic impulse' (which I long to refer to as Dicki), are you impressed? If told that it is (at the same time) a ray of the light of the Unborn, are you the more impressed?

But this we know; it is not the skandhas, or any of them. Nagasena's famous analogy of the chariot here applies. It is not unchanging and is therefore not an 'immortal soul'. It does not permanently distinguish between you and me. It is not the 'Spirit' of St Paul, the Life or Light which shines in every form or aggregate of forms. Nor is it his 'Body', in the sense of the personality. Is it his 'Soul'? Is this a reasonable term for the wayfarer on the Way, who trains unceasingly, with constant effort to become the More until, letting the Three Fires die, removing the Fetters and the Stains he 'enters the stream,' to become but a 'once-returner'?

It is clearly immensely complex, a mixture of qualities, in perpetual tension between the 'opposites' of the animal and the God which strive for mastery. E. J. Thomas in *The Life of Buddha* calls it a mere 'bundle of skandhas'. 'The ever-changing bundle of skandhas may be said to be new from moment to moment, and hence from birth to birth. But from birth to birth it remains a changing bundle, until it is finally dispersed with the extinction of craving.' In a later work, *The History of Buddhist Thought*, he goes on, 'But until this happens the individual is a being with a definite past which with a proper training he can remember'. Ananda Coomaraswamy calls it character, which I prefer, for is not character a highly complex, ever-changing aggregate of conflicting qualities all of which, as described in the first verse of the Dhammapada, are the product of the mind? And character improves with effort, being by no means confined to the skandhas. But 'You yourself must make the effort. Buddhas only point the Way'.

My thesis, then, is this. The Buddha taught Rebirth, of a complex aggregate which learns, from life to life, on the long road to Self-enlightenment. It is not the personality, the ego or self which includes Jung's 'shadow'. It is subject to *anicca*, change, *dukkha*, suffering self-caused, and is *anatta*, having no immortal and unchanging Self *which is its alone*. The Buddha's doctrine of Anatta, as distinct from the version taught today, is no impediment to the Buddha's doctrine of Rebirth.

He taught two selves, Atta and Non-atta ('Self is the lord of self') and both are manifestations, as all else, of the 'Unborn, Unoriginated, Unformed', the Parabrahman of Hinduism, the Spirit of St Paul. The Wayfarer, the evolving character, the 'psyche' of St Paul which is the subject of the psychologists, obeys the laws of nature as all else. All living things, and there is nothing dead, obey the rhythm of work and rest, of extroverted experience and introverted digestion of it. And this but reflects the outbreathing and inbreathing of the universe. Is man the sole exception to Nature's law?

In this I am of the Mahayana, which has never been troubled with this pother of choice between Rebirth and Anatta. I pity my friends of the Theravada as they vainly mutter 'No self, no self'. I prefer the freedom and joy of the universal process, its living unity with the Unborn whence it came. I know that the Self *is*, and that no thing is *not* Self in essence, and I know that Self, 'the Essence of pure Mind' as Hui-Neng called it, is the Buddha within, even as my skandhas, heavy with illusion, are not yet knowingly the Self—'herein is not the Self of me!' Let the Bhikkhu cry No-self at all; I feel that I know better!

We Live in Animals

The body old or young is animal
And through the orbit of enquiring eyes
The tenant-builder of the earthen form
Perceives, unwillingly, with dull surmise
A million other animals, the norm
Of human habitation. Bestial
Of birth, in borrowed skins enwrapt, erect
By long endeavour, man is still confined
To habits animal. What eyes shall see,
What sense of brooding immanence detect
The God alive within, the Buddha-Mind
That uses flesh to prove divinity?

Slave to an animal with Nature's own
Intent, man suffers, bound in pleasure-pain.
Then vision comes, the will to dispossess,
Brief moments of no-time as yet unknown
Of provenance. What now? Seek happiness
Or, riding on the bull, find God again?

APPROACH TO ZEN BUDDHISM

4

Beyond the Opposites

Few of us realize fully the dual nature of the world in which we live, and must live, for the duration of the universe. It is a world of duality, from all that we know of Spirit to all that we know of matter, and from it there is no escape for the personality of any man. Only consciousness, after lives of effort, can be raised to a level where duality no longer binds us, a Non-duality (Not One, not Two) which the Patriarch Hui-Neng called 'the Essence of pure Mind'. 'All distinctions are falsely imagined' as the same great man explained, whether subject/object, positive/negative, or the illusion of difference between Nirvana and the world of every day.

It is wise to approach the study of the Opposites at the point before they came into being. This lies in the field of meta-physics, of which physics is the material counterpart. We must begin with what the Buddha called the Unborn, and Hindus call THAT, for all attributes and epithets are vainly ascribed. From THAT came all we know or can know. First the One, but note that the One is not ultimate, in spite of the aspirations of millions of religious-minded persons. As a Zen Master observed when a pupil took refuge in this most comforting idea, 'And when all things are reduced to the One, to what is the One reduced?' How right he was, for even this One may as a concept be paired with the Many, and here is another of the pairs of opposites. But the One trembled and dissolved into Two. In the words of the Tao Te Ching, 'From eternal non-existence we serenely observe the mysterious beginning of the Universe. From eternal existence we clearly see the apparent distinctions. These two are the same in source and become different when manifested.'

Why the division? 'The bifurcation,' answers Dr Suzuki, 'subject and object, is needed to make us aware of consciousness.' Without it consciousness is mere unconsciousness. Nought can be conscious without that which is to it 'other'. Subject must look at object to know

53

itself. We can only know what we are not. Hence the famous example of 'Zen logic', that A must be seen to be not-A if we are to know A.

But Two is a concept impossible to use. It is, as Plato pointed out, a digit without meaning. Where there is two there must be relationship between them, and this makes Three. And in the arrangement of three things and their derivatives we attain the 'ten thousand things' of Chinese philosophy. Again, the Tao Te Ching describes the process perfectly. 'Tao begets One; One begets Two; Two begets Three; Three begets all things. All things are backed by the Shade (*Yin*) and faced by the Light (*Yang*) and harmonised by the immaterial Breath (*Ch'i*).' As Sri Krishna Prem, the English writer who became accepted as one of the holy men of modern India, writes in *Man, the Measure of All Things*, which is his own commentary on the Stanzas of Dzyan, on which H. P. Blavatsky based *The Secret Doctrine*:

'The field of manifest externality, in which we "live and move and have our being", is neither purely subjective nor purely objective but a blend of both. . . . This actual relationship is a pulsating exchange between the poles of being, the shuttle which weaves the "Web of the Universe". The forces which bring out the outflow and the inflow (*pravritti* and *nivritti*) are simultaneously upholding this fluctuating web of power. Deep in the Cosmic Heart the stress of attention falls first on one mode and a universe is created; then on the other mode and that universe is withdrawn. Deep in the heart of man the same stress turns outwards and we awake, then it turns inwards and we sleep.' (1st ed., pp. 339–40).

Let us look more deeply at these Opposites and the relationship between them, for strangely enough a clear understanding may be of vital consequence at any moment of the day.

The Absolute 'breathes out' and becomes the One-without-a-second. This divides, and it is too lightly assumed that the parts lie side by side as the parts of an apple cut in two. But it seems to be more correct to regard one partner in each pair as having extruded from the other. From the Absolute, for example, came the relative; from the Void or Emptiness all form ('all form is Emptiness'); from the Darkness came Light, as correctly stated in Genesis; from Spirit, matter.

This 'vertical' tabulation, as a change from the concept of side by side, helps one to understand the trinity used in a thousand forms each hour of the day. For we cannot move very far in our enquiry without coming to terms with what in *Concentration and Meditation* I called the Higher Third. We lightly speak of truth and falsehood, beauty and ugliness, good and evil. But above each pair is the apex of a triangle, a point of consciousness which includes and absorbs these pairs at the level of Truth, Beauty, and the Good. This Higher Third is the source of, the creation of, and the complete synthesis of its lower correlates. The lowest triangle is based on the 'ground' of manifestation; the highest lifts one to the One and the Many, above which is the One-without-a-second, and beyond that? Presumably THAT.

And the practical value of all this? It provides as nothing else an escape-hatch from the tyranny of the Opposites. Without it we should be shut below for the whole life-cycle of a universe, torn with perpetual tension and with no escape save a sterile middle way of perpetual compromise.

Accepting a Higher Third for every pair, however, we have a ladder of triangles, as it were, from lowest matter to Spirit itself, and nought to oppose our climbing save the fetters riveted upon our feet by our own foolish, separative thought.

Let us then face our folly and be done with it. As Huang Po says, 'All the Buddhas and all sentient beings are nothing but the One Mind, besides which nothing exists'. But we in our folly, using and misusing the magnificent instrument of thought, divide Reality and make it two. It *is* two, but it does not cease to be One! Eastern thought is filled with warning of this propensity of mind and the confusion and suffering which the habit entails. 'Mind is the slayer of the Real', says *The Voice of the Silence*. 'Let the disciple slay the slayer.' It is true that from the viewpoint of the Beyond of thought even Spirit and Matter are but aspects of the same Non-duality, but inferior mind reflects its superior parent disastrously. For it is one thing to watch the divine process of division without dividing; quite another to split that which is one into two and to lose sight of the still existing unity. Thought without intuition breaks all objects into a thousand parts with cold analysis. The intuition, using thought to analyse if need be, sees unwinkingly the Non-duality of which the severed parts have never ceased to be one. Bereft of the light of Buddhi, the lamp of the Light within, the mind falls into the 'great dire heresy of separateness that weans thee from the rest', as the *Voice* describes it. This is *attavada*, the heresy of the belief in a separate immortal Soul within the individual. This is the true doctrine of Anatta, that there is in man no unchanging faculty or principle which is not in truth an undivided part of the ultimate 'Unborn'.

So long as the student is immersed in this delusion of self he will seek in vain the Non-duality which is the 'self-identity', as Dr Suzuki calls it in many a volume, of the Beyond of here and now. In brief, 'Zen is not only thought but non-thought. It discriminates and at the same time holds in itself that which transcends discrimination.' (*Living by Zen*, p. 150). The former is the function of the intellect; the latter is that 'Medium-less perception' which is called intuition, as the same author says elsewhere.

Let us look yet again at the Opposites as a false reality to be used and then transcended. We see and feel the tension between them in every thought and action of the day. The highest, metaphysical pairs may seem beyond our immediate grasp, but lower aspects of these two, reflected down through the planes of manifestation, may either be seen as complementary opposites to one of which we are more or less attached at the moment, or as irritating opposition to our ego-will coming from a source which, as an opponent party in politics or a rival religion, should surely be abolished!

Human and divine, male and female, action-reaction, these are clichés. In philosophy we read of subject-object, affirmation-negation, cause-effect; in psychology of the conscious and unconscious, introvert and extravert, the intellect and the intuition. In all religion we find *jiriki*, salvation by self-power and *tariki*, by 'other'-power, and in Buddhism in particular the complementary ideal of the Arhat and Bodhisattva, of Prajna/Karuna, of the Self and Not-Self, so gravely misunderstood by those who claim that there is no self at all, even in Samsara. In the rhythmic alternation of nature we have the cycle of growth and decay, of day and night, of work and rest, and everywhere the conflict between part and whole, of the individual and the State and the troublesome problem of good and evil. But the list is endless, and we must wait awhile before we face, as face we must, the ultimate, mind-staggering Pair and its essential Non-duality.

In respect of all these opposites we can lay down four propositions, not as dogma but as facts available to all who examine life for themselves.

First, each of a pair exists by virtue of the other, whether as complementary opposites like positive and negative, or comparative attributes such as large and small. This is a profound statement, but understanding of it tends to ease us out of the false position in which we stand.

It follows that each opposite is partial, incomplete, both being needed for the least expression of truth. Hence the acceptance by religions and philosophies of a relative and an absolute Truth, the former pertaining to the realm of intellectual digestion and 'proof', the latter remaining forever beyond consciousness which has not climbed to its own level of No-thought, No-Mind in pure awareness. Even in the lower field of relative understanding this new view of the opposites will slay all dogmatism. How can any statement be the subject of worship or even of unchangeable conviction when the opposite claims attention as of equal right to be heard? And are not the opposites of 'right' and 'wrong' now suspect? At least they are relative to each other and much else.

Secondly, it does not need a profound sense of mysticism to see that each of the opposites *is* in a sense the other. At least we can see the two sides as closely as the two sides of a coin. And thirdly, each *needs* the other in order to be complete. This has profound importance in the field of psychology. Do we realize that we *need* the thing we hate, the aspects of the self we thrust into the unconscious as unworthy of the mask we offer to the world?

As a fourth proposition it is submitted that the tension inherent in duality, of attraction/repulsion working at full force on things, people and situations, is either accepted as the motive force of growth and development, or regarded as a source of suffering by those who cannot see it in this light. He who feels himself to be pushed about by the contending force between the opposites, and resents the pressure, will suffer by his resistance. But he who perceives and learns to use the flow of force to his own and the world's betterment will feel no suffering thereby. As a yachtsman uses the wind and tide to reach a chosen harbour, as a merchant alters himself with opportunity, learning to press this way or that or to wait upon the convenience of time, so the wise man, without complaint of circumstance, moves on the rhythm of natural force to achieve his end.

But the extremes of cosmic tension are most severely felt within the mind. On the one hand, the Life-force, flowing from the Unborn through every form or thing or event, uses all alike to its own high purposes; on the other hand the ego-self, the non-Atman or An-atta, blind with the illusion of separate existence and deaf to the voice of the Buddha-mind within, strives for self, and pitting its will against that of the universe is filled with suffering wrought of its purely personal desires.

We can now ask ourselves three questions. In every case where one of the opposites is dominant in the mind, can we genuinely see and actually express the other point of view? I was deeply impressed to learn of a debating society where no main speaker was allowed to support one side of a controversial motion until he had satisfied the committee that he could sincerely though briefly speak to precisely the opposite. What fun, if this were the rule in the House of Commons: or even in the Buddhist Society! Could the exclusive Theravadin student argue, apparently sincerely, the delights of Zen? Or vice versa?

A second question; Can we be truly tolerant of the 'other', that blithering idiot who insists on going straight to hell with his dangerous and quite horrible ideas? Probably not, but I remember a definition of tolerance given by Annie Besant nearly fifty years ago, 'an eager and a glad acceptance of the way along which our brother seeks the truth'. Yes, we *must* let him go the way he wills, for he will not learn from our admonishment. And a third question; can we choose and use the opposites yet not be bound by our choice? For of course we choose, a thousand times a day, be it only between two ways to the station. But are we slaves to a choice once made, in each of our daily habits? Can we change any one of them at will? Possibly not, for our conditioning of mind goes deep, and leads to our normal reaction to each event in a way which a close observer might predict with annoying accuracy. We are conditioned by our birth, sex, religion, education, environment, job and home. By our choice in politics, recreation and ambition. By our mental type and colour of our skin, by age and health and spiritual achievement. How difficult, then, to 'let the mind abide nowhere' as advised by the greatest minds of the East. We strive to 'walk on' with a load of thought-creation all the heavier for being quite unrecognized. And most of us are increasing the burden day by day.

Meanwhile the tension in which we live is inevitable and 'right'. To the extent that it is a form of suffering we make it so, partly by our futile search for what we are pleased to call happiness. But happiness is not only an impossible ideal; it is an unworthy one. He who is for the moment happy, meaning without immediate sense of suffering of mind or feeling or body, forgets with the blindness of the veils of self 'the great sea of suffering caused by the tears of men'. 'Can there be bliss when all that lives must suffer? Shalt thou be saved and hear the whole world cry?' One could amend this famous question from *The Voice of the Silence* by ending it, 'and fail to hear the whole world cry?'

There is indeed no escape from the tension of the opposites, neither in pleasure, in making money, nor in illness, suicide or death. But what any man can do, and what this 'approach to Zen' suggests that he should do, with profit to all mankind, is to rise in consciousness to the level where the tension exists and is profitably used, but the sense of suffering has vanished with the self within whose narrow world it once held sway.

How shall we find a condition of mind wherein both of each pair are included, digested, and used?

One can make suggestions. We can narrow the ambit of our waddle along the Middle Way, that moving centre between all extremes. As I brightly observed a long time ago, man walks upon two legs; we waddle from side to side of the median line, our weight upon this foot and then on that. Can we narrow that width, and so walk that much straighter and therefore beyond the pull of the divided force of the pair? We can apply the same principle to the working mind. In equanimity, even-mindedness, we refuse to be pulled or pushed to extreme opinion, like or dislike, point of view.

We can begin to raise consciousness to see the pairs, not merely in metaphysical theory but in daily life, as equally forms of the one indivisible Life-force of the Absolute Unborn in manifestation. We are thus approaching the moment when we shall see them *before* the bifurcation, the forking into duality, took place. If we can see the two sides of the penny we are less concerned whether the side be heads or tails.

We learn to see that all things, being children of the Unborn, are not only inter-related but inter-dependent. Verily 'we are members one of another', locked in an inseverable embrace which changes every moment under the sway of Karma, and moves to the More and so to the Most in a series of working 'days' which are the units of rebirth.

So now we are faced with the Beyond of duality, not as a far ideal still wrapped in fog but with understanding a little more advanced. With intellect strained to its limits we move towards the Unborn. But where is the bridge between thought and No-thought, duality and Non-duality? In a sense there is none, nor can there be. The Absolute is; we of the relative can neither add to it nor enter it nor take from it ought away. Yet we are part of it, we *are* it! It is immanent as well as transcendent; else could we never know that which we have never ceased to be.

Where is that bridge? The mystics have seen, so to speak, the other end of it, and move back to describe what they have seen. The leading scientific minds are now, surprisingly, approaching this end of it, moving out of the realm of matter to see that it does not exist. Energy, perhaps, or just events, no more. The gap is closing. True, as Professor Murti depressingly explains, 'the absolute and phenomena never stand on the same plain; they cannot be related, compared or contrasted'. But on the next page of *The Central Philosophy of Buddhism* he is more helpful. 'The Absolute is the *reality* of the apparent. Conversely, phenomena are the veiled form or false appearance of the Absolute.'

In the November 1969 issue of *The Middle Way* I described what I call 'Illumined Thought'. By profound study, in which the intuition is given full play, thought itself becomes illumined by the light of Buddha-Mind and we suddenly 'see', at first in 'peeps' and then with a great break-through, the world wherein all is still duality but the pairs are simultaneously seen as twin aspects of an inseverable reality. Here and here only is the solution to the problem of the bridge, *that none is needed.* As Nagarjuna, the greatest mind in the history of Buddhism has written, 'There is no difference at all between Nirvana and Samsara; that which is the limit of Nirvana is also the limit of the world. Between the two we cannot find the slightest shade of difference'. Dr Conze, in *Buddhist Wisdom Books*, p. 83, presses this home. That the Beyond is precisely identical with its opposite passes belief, and yet that is the message of the Heart Sutra. 'The infinitely Far Away is not only near, but it is infinitely near. It is nowhere, and nowhere it is not. This is the mystical identity of opposites. . . .'

What else can one say? The Opposites are, and ever will be for the period of our consciousness. But using the same consciousness we can, at first with intellect and later in the full knowledge of Prajna-intuition, learn to live in the world of duality while never ceasing to see that every two are one, that 'all distinctions are falsely imagined', that, as Dr Suzuki says, 'there is nothing infinite apart from finite things'. What new life is here released, what spiritual excitement for the days to come! Let me end with the immortal words of the third Patriarch in his poem, 'On Trust in the Heart':

> In the higher realms of true Suchness
> There is neither self nor other.
> When direct identification is sought
> We can only say, Not two.

Strange Discovery

I fret with trifles, uselessly discuss
Each truthless rumour of the world's affray;
Make furious plans of no importance; fuss
About the least disturbance of my day.
I want, appreciation. I demand,
Unfettered passage to my will. I grow,
To others' loss, and climb, until I stand
On pinnacles of self-engendered woe.
When Truth is enemy to self I lie;
Unless for profit why should I be kind? . . .

This horror bears two names, the first is I,
The second, less well-known, is Buddha-Mind.

5

If Life is One

All religions and philosophies make statements of doctrine which, by long use and repetition, become the worn coins of thought, and shine no more with the light of the experience in which that thought was born. If we can climb, however, just that much nearer to the direct experience, we find not merely thoughts encased in words but powerful forces, dynamic cosmic principles which, if welcomed fully in the mind, will, with the surge and thunder of a new awareness, burst the containers of old thought, set free the native powers of intuition and direct perception, and raise the whole man to a level of being hitherto unknown. There is, of course, a price for such attainment, and it is the deliberate, sustained digestion of the principle now seen as such, with constant study and perpetual application to the moment's circumstance.

Here, then, are two very different things, worn-out platitudes, and forces in the mind whose power is only limited by the mind's conditioning and the opposition of the ego, which knows that all such truths are enemies and that by their power it will inevitably die.

Such a thought principle is the statement 'Life is One', meaning thereby that the universal Life-force which operates on all planes and informs all bodies is one and indivisible.

One must approach the proposition from two points of view; first, is it true, and secondly, if so what happens or should happen in the lives of each of us. First, is it true? Can the opposite conceivably be true? Can one imagine a million million objects each exhibiting life, and such life having in each case a separate origin? Can the proposition be proved? No, but it has been well said that nothing worth proving can be proved. But let it loose in the mind, and the force of truth will prove itself, excitingly, uncomfortably, but beyond all argument.

Such final proof, intuitive experience, calls for a stiff climb to the heights of thinking and then the existential leap beyond the 'hundred-foot pole' of intellectual reasoning. We must climb much nearer to the home of Truth, the realm of Prajna-intuition as the East describes it. Let us climb.

At the top, at the highest point of human thought, is what the Hindus call THAT, and the Buddha, 'the Unborn, Unoriginated Unconditioned'. In the Parinirvana Sutra it is called 'the one principle of life which exists independently of all external phenomena'. The Taoists call it Tao, whence comes the One. Eckhart called it Gottheit, 'Godness' beyond God. It is the Namelessness with many names.

All agree that its first emanation is One, an indivisible unity which yet, in the process of manifestation, divides itself in two. Here is the one Mind-Only, Buddha-Mind, at the same time Noumenon/phenomena, Absolute/relative, Subject/object. Thence all the 'pairs of opposites', Darkness-Light, Negative-Positive, Affirmation and Denial. And the Two become Three (with the relationship between them), and thence appear what the Chinese call the '10,000 things'.

What mighty Force, Will, Energy drove THAT to become That/This? What Power 'breathed out', as the Hindus say, to become One-Two-Three and everything, while remaining itself eternally unmanifest? A power which creates, uses and then destroys by its very force all forms? Which is no-thing or nothing becoming all things? I shall call it Life.

This is the Spirit in matter, the Life in form ('Form is emptiness and the very emptiness is form'). The opposite of Life, if any, is form. It is not death. *There is no death*, only the cycle of birth, growth, decay and death inevitable in every form. 'The cause of death is birth'; it is as simple as that.

As Life is one, so is consciousness, which is equally indivisible and invisible. There is a cycle, of unconsciousness; consciousness ('I am'); self-consciousness ('I know that I am I'), and finally Nirvana (full consciousness without self-consciousness), the ultimate mystery which is the heart of Enlightenment.

But if THAT breathed out, as here described, while remaining THAT, then all about us, all Samsara is truly *maya*, the great Illusion. All things are real to each other yet, as Hui-Neng proclaimed, 'From the first not a thing is'. Here is paradox, wherein we are helped by the Diamond Sutra, 'There are no things or people, yet there are!' Applying this to the everlasting argument on self, which I submit to be quite unnecessary, the Theravada school is right in proclaiming the doctrine of Anatta, no-self, in the sense of no separate self or essence in any single thing; and the Mahayana school is equally right, in proclaiming that if 'Self' be the life of THAT there is nothing else!

But in Samsara man is dual, and at war, with intolerable tension in the mind. Bound in the toils of Samsara we wish to escape, to run away. We cannot, for there is nowhere to run away, and we need not, for if Samsara is the manifestation of the Unborn, Unconditioned, the Light is here and in us, and the task before us is but to see it so. But we must *see* it so. As Dr Suzuki has pointed out, 'the phrase One in All and All in One is to be understood as a complete statement of absolute fact, and not to be analysed into its component parts'.

Here, then, is the chosen thought-principle, that Life is one indivisible stream of consciousness, a living and intelligent force which is the Buddha-Mind in action. According to an old saying 'it sleeps in the mineral, wakes in the vegetable, moves in the animal and is self-conscious in Man'. For there is no such thing as dead matter, and science is rapidly proving, in the footsteps of the Buddha, that there is indeed no 'matter', alive or dead!

In every form it is the Life-force which makes that thing precisely what it is, its 'isness' or 'suchness' (*tathata*). I presume, therefore, that we may regard each 'thing' as a focal centre of the One Life at that moment in that form. A focal centre in the universal Buddha-Mind?

But as there is no final matter, as the splitting of the atom and all its ingredients has proved, but only Force or Energy—or Life—we too in our temporary bodies and inner sheathes and principles are but focal points in the same stream of consciousness.

If this be so, what is our relation with (*a*) the Unborn, and (*b*) each other? As to (*a*), the Unborn remains the Unborn even when manifesting in Samsara, as taught in all the great schools of mysticism, and the Buddha-Mind within each form is one with the Buddha-Mind. As to (*b*), we must learn the exciting but hard lesson that 'there are no others'. R. H. Blyth translates one of the didactic poems of Ikkyu to this effect:

> Deeply thinking of it,
> I and other people—
> There is no difference,
> As there is no mind
> Beyond this Mind.

And this Mind is that referred to by the Master Huang Po when he opens his famous volume with the words, 'The Master said to me: All the Buddhas and all sentient beings are nothing but the One Mind, beside which nothing exists'. How then is there room for others, save as part of the general illusion of Samsara, the relative world of untrue duality? But it is not enough to repeat quotations; we must rise to the level of the experience in which they are seen to be true. Then we can agree with another Zen master,

> When we are enlightened as to the selflessness of all beings
> What difference is there between my face and the Buddha's face?

Notice the keyword selflessness. So long as ego fights with ego there is no vision of the Self which is beyond, above and yet within both. We must somehow reach the stage when 'Self meets Self and recognizes itself in Other'.

This is mysticism, as agreed in all known schools. 'I and my Father are One', is a supernal saying, comparable with *The Voice of the Silence*, 'Look within; thou *art* Buddha'. Hence the advice is sound, whether in meditation or in daily life, 'Seek ye first the Kingdom of God and his righteousness, and all things shall be added unto you'.

Yet in a sense a thing can only exist if separate. A drop of water is not a drop of water while still part of the sea. From this fact derives the 'Zen logic' of no logic, to the effect that A is only A because A is also not-A, and vice versa. But here is the 'great heresy of separateness', the false belief that I in my form am 'really' separate from you in yours. For here is the ego, the true cause of suffering, and the whole Path is designed to root out this heresy.

Look more closely at your brother, this other thing that faces you in relativity. He may be your blood relation, a friend or enemy, your boss or your employee, of any colour, caste or creed. He is your brother, and you are his keeper, as he yours. You are both important/unimportant, and both suffering. As an Indian poet wrote,

> And in my brother's face I see
> My own unanswered agony.

You have both contributed to 'that mighty sea of sorrow formed of the tears of men', and know 'the still sad music of humanity'.

Try loving him. Patanjali says that love is a form of knowledge and that we truly know a person by becoming one with him in love. Few can say if this be true or not because few try it. Yet we must learn to hate not the man but his evil, and to help him bear the consequences of the latter. This means for you and me being vulnerable, a lowering of the ramparts of self. You helped to make him what he is, better or worse than yourself if you dare to judge. Your thought is changing him now as his is changing you. You both in equal measure share the Karma of mankind. The Stoic Emperor, Marcus Aurelius, wrote in

E

his diary, 'Enter into every man's inner self and let every man enter into thine'. This means to recognize in him as he in you the same Buddha-Mind, and R. H. Blyth is right as usual when he writes, 'The closer we are to Mind the closer we are to persons'.

So to part two of my thesis—If Life be One what follows? The multiple answer will be found in every mind in which the vast Thought-Principle is welcomed as a foretaste of enlightenment. Not only are we humans fully interrelated and utterly interdependent, but our Karma is as total as our goal is one. Life's total purpose is return—home, home to THAT whence into the illusion of space-time it came. Your purpose and mine, and that of all that lives is the same, to return, after many days, home. Here are days and nights of work and rest, lessons learnt and time for their digestion, for what is Buddhism without the reasonable and surely the inevitable doctrine of rebirth? I agree with lines from Dalmon's elegy for Edward Thomas:

> All feathered birds, and fishes finned,
> And clouds and rain and calm and wind,
> And sun and moon and stars, declare
> All life is one life, everywhere:
>
> That nothing dies to die for good
> In clay or dust, in stone or wood,
> But only rests awhile, to keep
> Life's ancient covenant with sleep.

How then does one apply in action the tremendous force now raging through both head and heart? How can one tabulate the observed effects of a totally new attitude of mind to all events and people? One can but mention a few as observed in oneself and fellow students of the like experience.

First, we can cease to blame others for any thing at all, whether they are in fact to blame or, as admitted in thoughtful analysis, we ourselves. In modern parlance we must cease to project. Just assume that it is all your fault. Make ego lie down and let the other do the projecting. It cannot possibly hurt you, and by refusing to project you have, in the view of Dr Carl Jung of Zürich done something to help mankind. In a famous passage in *Psychology and Religion* (p. 101) he describes the mechanism of these projections and the bravery of the man who begins to withdraw them. 'Such a man knows that whatever is wrong in the world is in himself, and if he only learns to deal with his own shadow then he has done something real for the world.

He has succeeded in removing an infinitesimal part at least of the unsolved, gigantic problem of our day.'

Secondly, surely the new awareness breeds a totally new tolerance of others' views and actions, even where they do not affect one's own. Can we not understand without disapproval? What my brother does and his way of doing it may be, for all we know, quite right for him, here, now. He too is 'working out his own salvation with diligence'. Should we not help him on his way to the one Goal as he sees it now? We may not approve of other schools or ways of life. Is it our business to inform these persons so? And if the same is applied to other Buddhist Societies it soon extends to people within our own. Is anyone else *quite* right in his Buddhism? But if Life be one. . . .

We shall learn to take this further, a long way further. As the poet Browning sang, 'God's in his Heaven. All's right with the world.' Who says that he is wrong? Or as the American poet Thoreau put it, 'I know that the enterprise is worthy. I know that things work well. I have heard no bad news.' Have you heard any, viewing it from the standpoint of the ultimate Unborn? In fact, as a Zen master put it, 'Every day is a good day', and he was speaking out of his enlightenment. It is a cosmic fact, if we can visualize it at that level, that 'It's all right', yes, all of it, for if any of it were otherwise the delicate harmony of the universe, the laws of Karma as the Buddha taught them, the perfect interrelation of all forms and circumstance, would alike explode in chaos. As a Zen master pointed out, 'the snowflakes fall, and each falls into its proper place'.

We can go farther still. If Life is one, and is an aspect or reflection of the ultimate 'Unborn, Unoriginated, Unformed', then all life is holy, if there is any meaning in that term, and every form of it. Ahimsa, non-harming, is indeed a Buddhist virtue, and travellers notice, as I did myself when staying in Buddhist lands, that these are naturally gentle people. Can we now look again at the bluebottle and the wasp we cheerfully destroy, at the thoughts in the mind which wills to destroy not only so-called pests but also those whose actions we deplore and would be delighted to see dead? Are we gentle of others' views, beliefs and differing ways of life? Their Life is ours and equally to be respected.

All these are small ways in which the newly awakened consciousness begins to function. It is still our consciousness, but the time comes when the one Life-force begins to speak as it were on its own behalf. This new master, the will of Life, which Sir Edwin Arnold called 'a Power divine which moves to good', at times takes over, and the individual becomes a conduit pipe for the flow according to its capacity.

67

But there is full co-operation, no negative mediumship; the servant obeys its lord and master, for truly 'Self is the lord of self; what other lord could there be?' (Dhammapada). But this is a matter of experience and not to be easily described.

And when the Life-force is thus absorbed and harnessed to the will, or, to be far more accurate, when the individual will is harnessed joyously to the very process of creation, another of these vast Thought-Principles appears on its own plane, where alone its full strength is absorbed. Compassion is now raised as far above affection as the no-self doctrine of the Theravadins was lifted by the Mahayanists into the field of Sunyata, the Void. The Bodhisattva now appears as far more vital than a vague ideal for worship. What else can a man become who sees all life as one, and all its human forms just so many beings bound in illusion and needing help to escape to their own Reality? Life as Wisdom (Prajna) now works out each moment of the day in Life as Compassion (Karuna) and the Wisdom/Compassion are inseverable. All that we learn and experience and find to be true is immediately and unceasingly at the service of all life in every form.

The Bodhisattva is complementary to the Arhat. 'In his wisdom he sees no persons; in his compassion he is resolved to save them. His ability to combine these contradictory attitudes is the source of his greatness.' Thus Dr Conze pithily sets out the ultimate paradox. All things are *sunya*, void. As separate things they do not exist. Yet all need saving, and the man who sees that Life is one is dedicated to that end. Perhaps Life itself is 'the love that passeth understanding', and that great Buddhist, Dr Suzuki, in his last talk with the late Father Merton expressed the view, 'the most important thing is Love'.

Perhaps our love for our brothers is the measure of our awakening. Jesus said, 'This commandment I give unto you, that ye love one another. By this men shall know that ye are my disciples.' May one paraphrase the later saying, 'Thou shalt love the Buddha-Mind with all thy heart . . . and thy neighbour as thyself'. Why not, if Life be one?

And now look up. Beyond the stars, the known and yet unmeasured universe, is what? Just Life, and its infinite forms. No self, no other. And Wordsworth saw each one of those forms with faces turned to the Unborn whence the born world of Samsara came,

> The joy I felt . . .
> With every form of creature, as it looked
> Towards the Uncreated with a countenance
> Of adoration, with an eye of love.

Perhaps we are nearer now to the mighty phrase at the heart of Zen. 'Live life as life lives itself.' To the extent that we succeed we shall meet in Heaven, and that Heaven will be here, and now, and doing this, with laughter in the heart and eyes of peace.

6

Illumined Thought

I have found, from increasing experience supported by the Scriptures and leading Buddhist minds that, although direct experience of Enlightenment is sudden, and not the *result* of any previous training, yet the individual, while still in a cocoon of concept, may so develop his faculties that he reaches an improved condition for the sudden 'break-through' to the Beyond of thought. If this be called gradual preparation for sudden enlightenment I have found it to be true.

In such development there comes a stage when the 'higher mind' is increasingly illumined, via Prajna-intuition, and the wall grows wafer-thin between knowing *about* and knowing, between 'seeing through a glass darkly' and 'seeing face to face', between *my* awareness of Reality and true Zen insight which is, as Thomas Merton called it, 'not our awareness but Being's awareness of itself in us'.

If this be true, I draw attention to it for the benefit of those who are tired of being told of the futility of striving to achieve enlightenment. There may be confusion here between the awareness of those who have 'arrived' and of those who have scarce begun to travel. For the latter the question is, what should we *do* to begin to move towards this high awareness ? These notes suggest an answer.

My thesis may be displayed in numbered propositions, each the fruit of study and that increasing pressure of the mind on a chosen theme, or none, which I call meditation.

1. Enlightenment, whether as flashes or a major 'breakthrough', is sudden and in itself complete. I accept Dr Suzuki's comparison between the Gradual and Sudden schools of Shen-hsiu and Hui-neng to the effect that 'the coming of enlightenment is instantaneous but the process of arriving at enlightenment is naturally gradual, requiring much time and concentration'. Yet I do not believe that a single experience should be called Enlightenment, and I agree with Hakuin

when he made the distinction, 'Six or seven times I had the bliss of passing through, and times without number the dancing joy (of minor Satori)'. In this sense, only the Buddha was the Fully-enlightened One.

2. However attained (or 'non-attained') this 'moment of no-time' does not arrive unless preceded by periods of intense effort, producing mental strain and consequent suffering. If there is any exception to this rule I should be interested to hear of it. Huang Po closed the Wan Ling Record with the words:

> Be diligent! Be diligent!
> Exert your strength in this life to attain,
> Or else incur long aeons of further gain!

And the Buddha's final words are recorded as, 'Impermanent are all component things. Strive mightily!' Strive for what, if not to realize that the Buddha-Mind is already within, that there is nothing to attain?

This striving seems to call for long self-training, and the Buddhist Scriptures are full of it. What else is the Noble Eightfold Path? What else is the koan exercise which occupies long years in a Zen monastery? The preparation may be long or short; the achievement will be the same. The quality of the smallest peep of the Beyond is unique and unmistakeable. Only its length and depth and the mind's power to return to it at will, vary with each experience.

3. Man is multiple. The five Skandhas describe the personality, and are truly Anatta, without any self which separates them from the ceaseless flow of the one Life-Principle which uses, but is not contained in, any form. But the Skandhas do not compose the man. There is here no mention of the will: 'The will is the man and Zen appeals to it' (Suzuki). No mention of Manas, the many-functioned mind, of Buddhi, the intuition, or of Atman. All are aspects of the total man and for total enlightenment all are needed.

In the West the paramount faculty today is the intellect. It is for most of us the means of communicating with the world around, and for discovering truth. But those most proud of this magnificent instrument are the least willing to admit its limitations. They refuse to understand that just as the range of the senses is narrowly defined, and feeling may be sharply distinguished from thought, so thinking is confined to its own field, wherein it learns more and more *about* phenomena. But thought can never *know*, in the sense of im-mediate, direct awareness. Thinking must reach the end of thought before the next faculty takes over. In nature there are no by-passes and no short cuts.

But the mind has many levels. The lowest is too often filled with ego-desire for the world of sense. 'Above' is the thought-machine of daily use, and for the few the faculty of higher thought, of noble, abstract thinking which ever moves to awareness of total unity. Upon this level I believe are great minds which as yet have no direct and conscious awareness of a definite break-through to Non-duality, but are yet illumined to an ever-increasing degree by the One-Light streaming down through the intuition.

4. But Manas functions, even at its finest, in duality. It acquires an intellectual awareness of Enlightenment. It understands that the Buddha-Mind is already within and that effort to attain it is in a sense both vain and unnecessary. On such a plane the Buddhist comes to terms with the great principles of Buddhist thought, the Void and Suchness, Wisdom/Compassion as inseverable, even the 'Unborn' and the fact that Nirvana is already here and now. But such awareness is still conceptual. No man by the intellect alone directly *knows* them to be true. Still there is an 'I' that sees and knows; not yet the seeing which is no-seeing.

5. Such direct, impersonal knowledge is of Buddhi, the 'built in', but for most of us still undeveloped, faculty of what Dr Suzuki calls Prajna-intuition. This seems to function as a receiving set in the mind for the still higher force of Atman, itself the property of no man. None owns the sunlight as it falls upon us, and the Atman in any man is but a flame of the Light which the Buddha called the Unborn. As Dr Suzuki says in *The Field of Zen*, 'To say there is no ego, no Atman, this is not enough. We must go one step beyond and say that there *is* Atman, but this Atman is not on the plane of the relative but on the plane of the absolute.'

6. But the faculties of man are not like the storeys of a house, divided. They are but 'forms of force', so many *upadhi*, vehicles or bases in an undivided stream of consciousness. They are utterly interrelated, and the total man, the universe in miniature, is a living whole of inconceivable complexity.

As, therefore, the light of Enlightenment, already shining in the higher mind, is, by deliberate purification and control, assisted to penetrate through man's descending, ever-denser vehicles of consciousness, it is not surprising to find that the next below Buddhi, if we may continue the vertical analogy, will be the first to be irradiated with the Light, often long before any break-through to im-mediate, direct at-one-ment with it.

I for one have found that by profound study, by what I mean by the word meditation, and by daily application, the thinking mind is increasingly opened to the intuition, and through its burning glass, to the Light of the Beyond itself.

7. Deep study of what the great ones say of the dozen or more tremendous themes which fill the higher ranges of Buddhism cause them to take root and work as yeast in the mind. The results are (a) to lessen attachment to all concepts, things and principles (including these!); (b) to reduce the ego-illusion in size and power; and (c) to produce that 'turning about at the seat of consciousness', that true conversion which provides in turn a profound change of values and thence the dedicated man. Into such a state of Mind will come, I believe, more readily the first moments of Satori or Prajna-intuition, a brief awakening to the Unborn.

8. Thus have I found, and to be told by those of great achievement, 'Just drop all concept', or 'Just see the Buddha-mind as that which alone exists', or 'Just see the folly of trying to attain what you already have', these phrases afford no practical help to the English mind. I answer, on my own behalf and for a thousand others, 'How?' What do I *do* as the first step to such awareness?

I hear these great ones say that the first step on the Zen path opens with the first experience. This splendid saying I accept as in one sense true, but we are here concerned with a preliminary path which leads, as all such paths must lead, to the Gate-less Gate at which occurs this first experience. I accept the old Buddhist saying, that 'the ways to the One are as many as the lives of men', but each of these ways approaches, via the moment of conversion, 'the turning about at the seat of con-sciousness', the first substantial Zen experience. Along these several ways, none better than another, the seeker learns what he seeks, develops the will to find it and in the darkness of Avidya probes for the Gate. Thereafter he marches through a land of paradox where no man marches upon no road and achieves no end of it.

Meanwhile, how do we help our brothers to move, by some way of their choosing, to the Gate-less Gate of true beginning? For I firmly believe that it is one's duty to 'Point out the Way—however dimly and lost among the host—as does the evening star to those who tread their path in darkness'. And the Dhammapada echoes *The Voice of the Silence*

73

in saying that 'Even Buddhas do but point the Way'. If it be true that a teacher has only one possession, a finger with which to point to the moon, shall we not point, for those who cannot see the moon?

My own pointing must be personal, for none can help save from his own experience.

I advocate a threefold discipline, self-imposed and steadily maintained. First, *Study*, profound, unceasing study, to the best of the mind's ability. A living teacher of high worth may be better than books, but can equally prove a bad substitute, partly because of the dangers of guru-worship, and partly because to hang on the words of another stimulates the illusion that Truth can be so obtained, as a starling takes a worm from its parents in the nest, whereas, alas, Truth can only be found within. The study of books tends to reduce these dangers, and a book can be carried for odd moments of the day. I could name a dozen works which, annotated and cross-referenced and digested with deep thought, will train the 'higher mind' to transcend its own limitations, and turn mere principles of doctrine into living forces in the mind.

There is of course the type which for a while at least is unconcerned with intellect, being still on some alternate way, such as that of feeling and devotion. But just as the intellectual type must sooner or later develop *bhakti*, devotion, the way of love, so must these at some time develop the abstract intellect, before the fully enlightened man appears.

The second aspect of self-discipline is *Meditation*, by which I personally mean deep concentration on some theme or living principle with intent to extract, with the help of the intuition, the last drop of its meaning. Thereby one can revive at least some glimmer of the actual experience that the writer had and is trying to convey. Many prefer for this a quiet place and regular times. I happen to have trained myself to be at it all the time and wherever the body may be. But see that, whatever method used, the motive is pure. As the Lama Trungpa brilliantly says, in *Meditation in Action*, when asked to sum up the purpose of meditation, 'Meditation is dealing with purpose itself. It is not that meditation is for something, but it is dealing with the aim', which goes a long way towards Zen 'purposelessness' as the only right and proper purpose for doing anything at all. In the sense that I use the word meditation here the purpose is clear, for it is to train the mind to the death of self, and when self is dead the Unborn alone remains.

And third, *Application*. In facing a crisis, large or small, do we at once apply our Buddhist principles; the laws of Karma, the fact of

Sunyata, the delicate balance of Prajna/Karuna, the unreality of the 'I' that is getting so excited and upset? If not, why did we enter Buddhism?

So much for basic preparation. Only when so much is done, and thoroughly, do I find that much of it can be safely undone. One must, for example, in the final approach to Zen begin to control thinking to the point of stopping thought. But can one learn to stop thinking before one has learnt to think? Or to 'let go' before one has realized that one is heavily attached? Or to accept that the Buddha-Mind is all that IS before one has the least idea what it *is*? I do not believe so. Let the higher climbing wait until the lower slopes are with enormous effort gained.

In the face of knowing smiles from my youngers and betters I hold to my thesis, for I find it works. Think, I suggest, as hard and long and high as your intellect can manage, and rather more. Watch, how moments of understanding come which thought alone could not provide. Note, how the whole mind is more and more suffused with the light of certainty, serenity, of *knowing* what is true. The rest will come. And *then* you will say, as we all say on these occasions, 'How simple it all is! Of *course* all form is emptiness, all emptiness is form; of *course* Samsara is Nirvana, and all *is* the Buddha-Mind!'

Now you can begin your study in Zen. Walk on!

7

The Wisdom Gone Beyond

No philosophy, religion or system of spiritual training is born in a vacuum. In each case the spiritual experience of a man or group of men condenses into a tradition, with its own literature, great names and great ideals. The same is true of the specific form of condensation. In each case it is not too difficult to trace its genesis.

Ch'an Buddhism was born of Bodhidharma and Hui-Neng, who adapted Indian Buddhism to the Chinese mind. Their message was largely a repudiation of the written word in favour of 'direct seeing into the heart of man'. What irony, that the background without which it is difficult to understand the masters and their remembered words, is one of the largest and most exalted bodies of literature yet produced by man!

Zen itself of course needs neither literature nor formulated methods of approach. It is we who need guide-lines, 'fingers pointing the Way', to help us up the mountain side. The guide-lines here, the steps up which to climb the '100-foot pole' from which to leap into a new awareness, are contained in the literature of the *Prajna-paramita* (Prajna, the *Wisdom* which *beyond is gone*), and we must come to terms with it and its central theme of Sunya-ta, empti-ness, before our study of the Zen masters, their sermons and sayings can even be lightly understood. The connection could not be closer. As Dr Suzuki puts it bluntly, 'Zen developed from the intuitions of the Prajaparamita'. But note that Zen develops from its intuitions, not its concepts, its formulated thought. For we shall not understand the contents of the literature so long as we regard them as scholastic formulae. These are not intellectual propositions but collated attempts, by a long series of men of high spiritual attainment, to write down on the highest intel-lectual plane something of their own direct, im-mediate experience of Prajna-Wisdom, the waking in each of the same 'third eye' of Prajna-intuition. That is why Dr Suzuki says, 'To understand the Prajnaparamita we must entirely abandon what may be called the "this side" view of things and go over to the "other side". This "this side" view is where we generally are, where a world of discrimination and particulars extends. The shifting of this position to the "other side" of Sunyata . . . is a revolution in its deepest sense. It is also a revelation.' No wonder, he adds, that the new point of view is full of paradox and irrationality. The moment of this crossing to the other shore is conversion, the experience referred to in all religions. 'Let one remain at this side of dualism and the gap between relativity and Emptiness can never be bridged. . . . Sunyata is realized only after the "turning-over" in the Alayavijnana', the universal unconscious which is the basic theme of the Mind-Only school of Indian Buddhist thought.

The approach to the Void is difficult, and Dr Conze, the greatest Western authority on the subject, in his *Selected Sayings from the Perfection of Wisdom* sets a high standard for the student attempting that approach. He should be familiar with the Theravada scriptures, he says, and have a marked preference for intellectual methods of approach with an inclination to metaphysical thinking. He should 'have gained a fair measure of detachment from the things of the world', for only this will make possible a 'reorganization of all his motives and interests. Above all he must have a longing for the Absolute.' Let us not despair. Let us at least approach, for only thus shall we understand the Diamond Sutra, the Heart Sutra, the Blue Cliff Records and the Mumonkan.

Let us see what is this literature, what it says and how we should use it. To see what it is involves a few words of Buddhist history. We know that Buddhism was born in India in the sixth century BC and that after the Buddha's death there were a number of councils convened to discuss and agree the Dharma, the Teaching. We know of what came to be called the Hinayana School, whose eighteenth sub-sect survives today as the Theravada, with its canon complete in Pali. We know that there arose, remarkably soon, other schools or developed teachings and these, so to speak, moved off down the spokes of a wheel in very different directions. There was Nagarjuna's negative analytic attack on all phenomena which led to our present theme, the Void. We know of the complementary later school of Yogacara, of Vijnanavada or Mind-Only, which was more psychological, and set up the basic theme of the Universal Unconscious of Alayavijnana, the Store-Consciousness, seen from which all manifestation is non-existent, for all that exists is Mind-Only. The Mahayana doctrine of the Bodhisattva, complementary to the Theravada's ideal of the Arhat, was fully developed in the immensely popular Lotus Sutra, and the cult of Amida, developed in China, produced the Pure Land school of salvation by 'Other Power' which became popular in Japan as Shin. Later still came the Tantra of Bengal as adopted extensively in Tibet and thence in China and Japan. All these, and many more, are parts of the vast field of Buddhism, yet out of them the scriptures of the two first, the Madhyamika or Middle Way School associated with the mighty genius of Nagarjuna, and the Mind-Only School of Asanga and Vasubandhu, are of vital interest as the intuitive-intellectual background of Zen.

According to Dr Conze the Madhyamika school was born in South India about 100 BC and was thereafter developed in scriptures, summaries of those scriptures, and commentaries upon them for another four hundred years, much of the development taking place in the great university of Nalanda. The bulk of the Sutras is enormous, the commentary adding as much again, and only a small part has yet been translated. For most of us the Diamond Sutra and Heart Sutra, translated with commentary by Dr Conze in his *Buddhist Wisdom Books*, will here suffice. Its theme throughout is the Unconditioned, the Absolute, the Void of all predicates of every kind, the Emptiness which is empty even of emptiness.

Yet all this writing is desperately practical. The Heart Sutra itself is, as Dr Conze makes clear, an analysis of the Four Noble Truths in terms of Sunyata. As he puts it, 'Emptiness is not a theory, but a ladder that reaches out into the infinite. A ladder is not there to be discussed but to be climbed. . . . Its meaning will unfold as we climb.'

Let us climb. What does the doctrine of Emptiness say? That all things, all forms, all beings are in a constant state of flux. That none has *swabhava*, its 'own' being, in the sense of a separate essence making it different from other things and beings. That the doctrine of Anatta is true not only for your 'self' and mine but for all other things. Thus Sunyata has been described as 'merely Anatta taken to the nth degree.' That in a world of relative duality no doctrine and no statement can be entirely true. It can never be more than partly true, and its truth can be analysed and as such destroyed.

Can we on the strength of this take heart and see that of any 'thing' it is fair to say that it isn't there? This table, house, landscape, doctrine, noble ideal, just is not there! To a mind that has freed itself from attachment to the things of sense without, and the thoughts within, there is no thing left in existence. Was not Hui-Neng right in saying, therefore, 'From the first not a thing is'? But this remorseless and entire negation is not merely negative. A complementary positive is implied. 'The doctrine of Sunyata is not pure negativism. It is simply seeing things in their suchness. It does not deny the world of multiplicities. Mountains are there; cherries are in full bloom, the moon shines brightly in the autumnal night; but at the same time they are more than particularities, they appeal to us with a deeper meaning, *they are understood in relation to what they are not* (italics mine).' Here is the secret, and let us mark it well.

But Nagarjuna's attack on phenomena had to be negative; the process set out in Phase One of the Society's course just has to be applied. 'To be master of oneself', says Dr Suzuki, 'means to have the way thoroughly cleansed of all obstacles that may thwart the free self-governing course of the Prajna. Negation is this cleansing.' We begin by seeing most of our thoughts as no longer worth attachment. We end by seeing that there are no thoughts, nor thinking, nor any being to think!

Approaches to the fact of Emptiness are multiple. Each, or a blend of all, can be used as a step on the way to 'seeing' that 'all Form is Emptiness and the very Emptiness is Form'. When the 'moment' of seeing comes we laugh. Of course it is! But how do we reach this laughter? We must learn to live with nonsense, which is non-sense. As Dr Conze puts it, contradiction in this literature is piled on contradiction. 'Whatever is said about the Absolute gives really no sense but people feel the mental need to say it. The Prajnaparamita expresses a state of intoxication with the Unconditioned, and at the same time it attempts to cope with it, and to sober it down.' As we can observe for ourselves, every conditioned thing is what it is by virtue of its relation to something else. None has any exclusive existence. Each has its suchness, *tathata*, 'isness', which makes it what it is, but the suchness is void and indivisible. Perhaps it is the universal voidness applied to separate things. If we strip from any thing all its predicates and adjectives, all that can be said of it, what is left is utterly no thing or nothing, emptiness. Each thing is only a conglomeration of predicates, supplied by us, and has no existence without them. Yet while detaching ourselves from things and thoughts as having 'no abiding substance' or reality, we need not despise them. They must be treated and used as real, for we too exist in the illusion of duality. The difference is that we must learn at the same time to exist in non-duality. Then only can we wisely *use* these unreal, dual things.

The Void, then, is not a crater at our feet, a hole to be avoided; nor is it a new god to be worshipped with a wonderful new name. Rather it is an adventure of the spirit to perceive it, a new view of all things, of that without which they would not be as they are. Indeed, as Prajna, Wisdom, and Karuna, Compassion are one-not-two, all striving for perfection, the Unconditioned, is applied among men on the highest levels of the Bodhisattva ideal. 'The individual becomes perfect when he loses his individuality in the All to which he belongs.' Great words of Dr Suzuki, whether applied in the East or West. We must indeed hold fast to this rising sense of non-separation, that indeed 'all duality', as Hui-Neng says, 'is falsely imagined'.

This new awareness bears no name. The West cuts Truth into fragments which are apt to die as such. We study ontology, metaphysics, philosophy, psychology, mysticism, religion, morality and subdivisions of each. Are these just false divisions of the Indivisible or aspects of one Truth? At least we can approach the Void on ascending storeys, as it were, of the palace of Truth. In this analogy science is on the ground floor of physical matter. This table is built up on a billion billion atoms, each when split revealing molecules, neutrons and so on like Chinese boxes within each other composed of a minute quantity of matter surrounded, comparatively speaking, with oceans of space. But if each of these items is subdivided indefinitely what is left but force or motion, lines of energy which, crossing, produce the appearance we know as an event? Can we not say that the table just is not there?

Let us rise to the plane of philosophy, the intellectual manipulation of concepts in an attempt to reach a Truth which concept alone, says the Buddhist, can never attain. The Yogacara School, with its teaching of the Alayavijnana is concerned with Mind-Only, which Huang Po echoed by saying that 'All the Buddhas and all sentient beings are nothing but the One Mind, beside which nothing exists'. The West arrived at the same point with its school of Absolute Idealism. The mystics follow, or precede. The part is nothing save as merged in the Divine Whole, and vision is to see their self-identity. All these are surely saying that what we see is empty, illusion, just not there.

The dual doctrine of the Theravada, of Anicca/Anatta tells the same story. No thing is permanent; each changes with the speed of the thought which views it. 'There is no abiding principle in any thing', and none in any self. If there is none in the part there is none in their totality. Psychology joins the chorus, and the deep analysis of the Abhidhamma of the Theravada School works on the unreality of all phenomena and is echoed by the modern West. 'All that we are is the product of what we have thought', says the Dhammapada, and the West is beginning to agree. Again, it has been said that Zen is the child of Bodhidharma and Taoism. If so, look again at the eleventh chapter of the *Tao Te Ching*.

> Clay is moulded into vessels,
> and because of the space where nothing exists
> we are able to use them as vessels.
> Doors and windows are cut in the walls of a house
> and because they are empty spaces we are able to use them.
> Therefore on the one hand we have the benefit of existence
> and on the other we make use of non-existence

L. C. Beckett, whom we know in the Zen class as Mrs Lucille Frost, in *Neti, Neti* and two further works compares the recorded findings of modern astronomers with passages in the Lankavatara Sutra, the classic of the Yogacara School, and follows the same theme of the 'nothing between' into modern physics.

The Zen masters, in their maddening 'Zen logic' speak of thinking which leads, with the waking of Prajna-intuition, to *mu-shin*, No-Thought, No-Mind or Buddha-Mind.

But even the Void is an extreme, and that which is utterly empty must at the same time be utterly full. Yet the negative approach, that all is empty even of emptiness, is easier to grasp than its opposite, that all is full, that every smallest part is indeed the whole. Use nevertheless, if you wish, the positive approach of viewing all things in their such-ness, is-ness, *tathata*, by which each thing is precisely what it is. Just as in utter emptiness the seeming born remains Unborn, so in the suchness of each thing the Unborn is totally born. And the two are One in Non-duality (Not One, not Two). Thus the Void is empty but the Void is full. In brief, Sunyata, as I understand it, is to the Absolute as suchness is to each thing, which we now see just as it is. What is it? Unborn/born, Absolute/relative, Empty/full.

Has all this been too difficult, as an attempt to build a bridge between the known and the Unknowable? Surely the enormous effort needed to open the Prajna-eye, and to see that this noisy turmoil about us is indeed the Buddha-Mind in action, is well worth while. As Dr Suzuki puts it, and he should know, 'Contradiction in life is so deep-seated that it can never be eradicated until life is surveyed from a point higher than itself. When this is done the world of the Gandavyuha (the Void) ceases to be a mystery, a realm devoid of form and corporeality, for it now overlaps this earthly world; no, it becomes that; "Thou art it", and there is a perfect fusion of the two.'

From Brighton Pier

Lean over Brighton pier.
Observe the waves that rise and fall
And each the product of its neighbour.
See on this one suddenly a spume
Of blue-white water dancing happily
Unpurposed on the undivided sea.
It has, in form and size and colour
Beauty of its own. It dies, dissolves,
Its wetness, blue-and-whiteness, all its self
Returned to vast undifference.

What made it so,
What blend of moon-led tide and ocean-thrust,
And vagrant windy sky forged once
With fused uncertainty of power
That sunlit wavelet on a dancing sea?
And I, that pondering observe,
What provenance have I?
A million moments, born of No-thing were,
And being so, just this am I.

But who is this that speaks of this?
Who watches both observer and the sea?
He knows the wavelet of his name and form;
Content and happily diffused he knows
Himself no separate thing. Then whence the sea?

It is no matter; in the mind set free
There is no-wavelet dancing on no-sea!
No-Self to tell no-self it shall not be!
Only the dancing pier, the happy wave and me!

8

Living in Now

The theme of Living in the Now involves time, and the relation of its constituents, past, present and future, together with the law of causation which operates within them. It may be viewed on three levels.

Highest, of course, is the famous phrase 'the eternal Now' as developed by the greatest mind the West has produced, Eckhart. He would not have heard of the earlier Zen phrase, the 'one thought-moment' which is also beyond the reach of human time, and is still for most of us a mere concept. There is a middle level, that Now is all we need to trouble about, all that we need to know, even though in a sense the very concept of the present is illusion. On yet a third level it is one's *dharma*, in the Buddhist sense of duty, within the vast field of causation in which we pass our days. From this point of view it is the job in hand, and the importance of carrying it out with the total man and rightly; in other words, right action, a phrase which covers the middle section of the Buddha's Noble Eightfold Path.

Now the means of acquiring direct knowledge are only two, and our other faculties are concerned with making use of the knowledge so acquired. The first way is through the senses. If I put my hand into very hot water I have direct experience of the fact, and react accordingly. The same applies to all that we see or hear or taste or smell. This is direct experience. The only other means of direct knowledge is through a faculty still scorned by science but known to the East as Buddhi, the intuition. By this we have direct experience of things as they are, beyond the reach of the senses, as of thought and feeling. Between these two, sense perception and intuition, lies the process of digesting the experience so gained. There is no such thing as 'direct thought', in the sense of giving us anything new, save new ideas or feelings about our total experience. Students of Jung will remember his diagram of the four faculties of the mind, in which the intuition and the senses face the 'digestive' processes of thought and feeling.

This curious knowledge is of importance in right action. Sense-reaction should be simple and im-mediate. As a Zen master said, 'When hungry I eat, when tired I sleep', with no elaborate mental process in between. If the sunset is glorious why not enjoy it, instead of spoiling enjoyment with thoughts about it or attempts to describe it, to oneself or others ? Intuitive awareness, at the top end of the mental spectrum, as it were, is its own authority, and though thought may follow it will do so at the expense of the original experience.

Now man is at least dual, a god in an animal. The animal is obvious, and its needs should not be ignored. The god is not so obvious, but for the animal which is man, as distinct from those not so evolved, there is a 'beyond', of the senses, of the thoughts and feelings, to the God within who is sensed through the intuition. This is the Buddha-principle—'Look within, thou *art* Buddha'—part of the ultimate 'Unborn, Un-originated, Unformed'. As we learn to recognize this light of Buddha-hood we see the same in others, and sense, on one plane or another, our common divinity. But so long as we remain ignorant of this shared, undying principle we fight, individually and collectively, like animals, and take the consequences. Progress, therefore, is largely removing the veils which prevent us seeing this central and all-important fact.

Meanwhile the God-animal, who has been called the pilgrim of eternity, was born a very long time ago and will not return to 'his Father's home' for a very long time to come. But the Unborn, in terms of our time, just *is*. All else is moving, on the endless cycle of becoming. But the Goal is but a vague idea to most of us. What matters is the moment, the all-sufficient moment of Now which is reflected in each moment of the clock. This is enough and for most of us more than enough, for it postulates a vast amount of 'moments' arriving for our full attention every twenty-four hours.

All this is of prime importance on the subject of Now. For the Buddha refused to discuss Ultimates: he taught a Way, and spoke unceasingly of a wayfarer in training for the Way. For him the Way, and each moment of it, is itself the Goal. And it is surely true that we can but live now, and here, and spend our time in doing this. At the moment it is now; when you go home it will be now. Tomorrow it will be now. When is it other than now ? And it is always here. Have you ever been any other place than here, though 'here' may differ breath by breath ? And have you ever done anything else than this, what you are doing now ?

So we *can* but work here, doing this, now, and it is sad that so few of us are content with it. Yet this fact has its paradoxical converse. For there is no such time as the present. You came into this room in the past. The beginning of my talk is now past. So is the breath you have just expelled. And when you go home tonight, that is of the future. So is my next remark to you, and the breath you are about to draw. Then where is the present that is neither past nor yet to come? It is but a notion, a useful habit of thought for providing the context, as it were, of our action—now.

The Buddhist has all time for now. We were not born when our bodies were born, nor do we die with them. We shall not gain Enlightenment in a month or two, or a year or two, though we may achieve some minor break-through to better understanding of what this word may mean. We can therefore plan the next thing to be done in the greatest detail, and neither a god nor a devil shall prevent us. Just what is reborn day by day and life by life is to the wise man immaterial. But rebirth every moment, every day, and life by life is a necessary corollary of Karma, and the Buddhist scriptures are full of it. So is the religious teaching of the East from time immemorial.

But while we walk on, along this clearly defined but difficult Way, let us walk upright, in the now of posture, if such a phrase be acceptable. Most of us are leaning forward on to some authority, a person, teaching or book. If yours were suddenly removed would you not fall on your face for want of it? Nor should we lean back, on memories of the past, wishing that things would not change so rapidly. It is equally foolish to lean sideways, to rely on friends and those about us. The Buddhist treads a Middle Way, striving to oscillate from side to side, in like and dislike, hope and fear, a little less each day.

We must, in brief, be independent now and here as we are busy doing this, yet we are at the same time interdependent, for none of us walks alone. Each is affected by all that all others are doing anywhere in the universe. We are total, and it is folly to believe that we are not. The greatest illusion is the 'great heresy' of separateness, lost in which we nourish the illusion of a separate 'I'. We are at all times one, yet living in an ever-changing relationship with all others. On the one hand, we should mind our own business, which is a whole-time job; on the other, we are aware of the needs of others as they arise. All suffering is in a sense my suffering, and I have added to it by my folly. In every action now, therefore, we should strive to reduce the amount we cause, and cure as much as we can. In this there is no sacrifice. 'There is no such thing as sacrifice: there is only opportunity to serve.' All Buddhist schools are agreed on this, though the ideal man of the Theravada School, the Arhat, and that of the Mahayana, the Bodhi-

85

sattva, seem very different. In fact they are complementary. Whose mind can I control, improve and lead to enlightenment, save mine? Yet how can I climb the long road to the spirit's Everest if I am only concerned with 'me'? And though it sounds very noble 'to live to benefit mankind', indifferent to thought of self-enlightenment, can we supply such benefit with minds still uncontrolled, still sunk in the darkness of the heart's ignorance?

Let us begin to apply these principles. First, we must learn to accept what comes to us, completely, willingly. At present we resent what we do not like; are annoyed at what causes suffering; project, as the psychologists say, on to everyone else the blame which lies in ourselves and, generally, refuse to accept the consequences of folly. Yet it is right that we should suffer precisely as we do; the very universe would burst asunder if it were not so. In brief, we must begin to face the most difficult thought in the field of Buddhism, that 'It's all right', all of it, entirely all of it. Thus and thus only should we face each situation, just as it is. If we merely wish it were something different, how can we do what needs to be done and do it well? We must learn to withhold our perpetual like and dislike, our doubt as to whether it is what it ought to be. We must learn to say YES to everything, whatever it may be. It may be horrible, unbearable; men made it so, and we are men. If there is this to be done, let us do it, instead of telling our neighbour to do it, or explaining loudly what 'they' ought to do. But before we act at all let us be sure that it is our business to intervene. How many people worry about some war at the other end of the world in order to escape from the worry and war within? We are all at war, and shall be for a long while to come. There will be war in every mind until its cause is removed, and that is duality. The 'opposites' are in perpetual tension, and we with them. Only he who rises above this tension, accepting both opposing factors entirely and simultaneously, can bring what all men say they long for, peace, into his mind.

For peace is equilibrium, harmony, and the total law, a living and intelligent law, which the East calls Karma, strives to maintain it. Let us look again at Karma and its corollary, Rebirth, not as a form of cosmic accountancy but in terms of cosmic harmony destroyed and restored. For the primordial Absolute is born, in a cycle of becoming inconceivable in range, as a manifest totality or One. This, there being no other, is in perfect harmony. But man, when the One has become two in a million pairs of opposites, and the Two through Three becomes the multiplicity we know, is left—the story is too long to tell—with such freewill as he has not fettered with his previous action. In that freewill he burns himself in the 'three fires' of hatred, lust and illusion, of which illusion is the cause of all. But if Karma is indeed harmony, the man who by his action breaks it pays. Who else should pay? Is this not justice? That the breaker of the cup shall mend it, the disturber of the harmony make good the damage done? And if he calls the process suffering, that is his affair.

If this be so then all that happens truly happens 'right'. If you wish to make it better use your own mind now. As Omar Khayyam wrote,

> Ah, Love, could thou and I conspire
> To change this sorry scheme of things entire,
> Would we not shatter it to bits and then,
> Remould it, nearer to the heart's desire?

Well, why not get on with it? No one is stopping you!

But if all is right, looked at from a cosmic point of view, it is well to do each thing to be done as rightly as possible. May I give an example of the perfect act? You are walking to the station with a friend. Someone in front drops his umbrella, and as you come to it you pick it up and hand it to the man who dropped it. You then walk on, still talking to your friend, and in two minutes have forgotten the whole incident. Here is the perfect act—no motive, no desire for gain, no thought of self. The right time, place and means—and you have forgotten it! How nice if every action could be done that way.

Sometimes duty is not clear; we have a problem as to which of two courses to pursue. May I proffer my own experience? There is one factor you can remove from the problem, as a thorn with a pair of tweezers. It is self. How often there is then no problem at all. The trouble was that you saw quite well what you should do, but self wanted the opposite! Remove self and you remove the problem, at least as to seeing what ought to be done. What you then do is your concern, and your karma.

But no act, right though it be in time and place, in means and manner, is right if done with the wrong motive. I firmly believe that *why* we do each thing is more important than all other factors in what is done.

In the long view all is right action that serves the common weal, in the ultimate sense of the high purpose of the universe, and all is wrong that strives for personal ends that are incompatible with these. This is impossibly high for us, but it is worth remembering as a touchstone of right action.

And when some action, in the conscious now, done 'mindfully', as the Buddhist scriptures say, is done, can we then drop it? Or do we hold a long post-mortem, thinking, 'I ought to have done this instead'? Or, worse, do we blow up the balloon of the ego with self-praise? If there is self in it, there will be results, or good or bad, as we regard them so. If there is no self in it, there is no karmic debt to be paid, and one can the better understand the saying, 'The perfect act has no result'. Why not? For there was no actor!

You will find that living in the now abolishes regret, and for the future abolishes fear. For who regrets and who is afraid? The answer may prove helpful. Yet we must be sensible. We need not be feckless by living happily in now. If we are planning for the future we are planning now because now is the right moment for the job. But we need not live in the future of things planned or feared, nor in the past with vain regret.

Assume, then, that we now appreciate the ambit of the moment, the next step on the long march from what we are to what we would be. Here is the long Between in which we can but speculate unprofitably about the End. Of more importance, all importance, is the job in hand, now, here and doing this, whatever next seems right to be done, as best we may. Thus only shall we reach, at first in 'moments of no time', the Beyond. For within duality, here in Samsara, is to be found, if ever, the meaning of Nirvana, and when that moment comes it will be seen as Now.

9

London Zen

In 1967 the difficulties inherent in attempting to adapt the methods of Zen training of Japan to the needs and conditions of the English mind began to emerge, and to reach a stage of formulation. The first move was from Japan when an English visitor, ripe with years of meditation in a Japanese monastery, was heard to say that the Zen Class, which I had conducted on much the same lines since 1930, was not a class in Zen. I replied that that might well be true for it never has been a class in Rinzai Zen, which involves the use of the koan under an enlightened teacher, nor in Soto Zen which has not yet found a body of interested students.

But the criticism called for self-examination, which I conducted before the Class, and at their request published the result as 'London Zen' in *The Middle Way*, the journal of the Buddhist Society. It may be helpful to reproduce it here, as the last of the chapters on Zen Buddhism and as a useful prelude to those which follow.

I have, I repeat, heard it said of the Zen Class, which I have conducted on approximately the same lines since 1930, that it is not a class in Zen. This may be true, nor would I trouble to disagree. It is not a class in Rinzai Zen, if this implies the use of the koan, for the koan is not used. Nor is it a class in Soto Zen, for I know so little of Soto Zen that I could not teach it.

What is Taught?
What, then, do I teach? In one sense the answer is that of any teacher of the inner life—myself, and it is the ill-fortune of the class that its karma does not permit a better teacher. But spurred by the observation that the class should not be labelled Zen I gave much thought to the question, 'What do I teach?' For me the answer is reasonably clear,

and as I am asked by the class to do so I have no objection to putting it in print.

Though I do not advocate the use in London of the matured tradition of either of the Zen Schools of Japan, I profoundly admire the deliberate 'no-methods' of the early Patriarchs of China, who dealt with each pupil or enquirer according to his needs. And I admire the virile, even violent handling of each pupil, whereby the master is determined to make him find the Light within by his own efforts, and this in spite of the pupil's loud desire to be 'saved' by scriptures, sermons, sayings and the personality of a more developed mind.

What is Zen?

What, then, is Zen? For me it is a state of consciousness beyond duality. This I have known: this others I have met have known, and many of my class in the years gone by have known, in quality, duration and repetition varying with each. The experience is not mysterious, holy or particularly rare, though the 'great experience' is quite exceptional. But each, or great or small, is unmistakable, unforgettable and in-communicable by normal means. The 'peeps' of non-duality achieved, often without reference on the conscious plane to any effort recently made, are the beginning of the Zen path, hints that the seeker is searching in the right direction, and no more. For the Goal is the full develop-ment of the total man, on all of his seven planes, and even the Zen master has a long way yet to go.

Right Motive for the Search

How do we experience Non-duality? I answer by enquiring, *Why* do you seek it? For me right motive is more than a prime necessity; it is half the Path in itself, for he whose motive is utterly pure is largely free of self, and for such a one even 'the Gateless Gate' will open easily. I believe that without a developed thinking mind, a strong will and some intuitive vision Zen will never arrive, but even if it does it will arrive disastrously if the effort made was the product of wrong motive. God help the man, if God there be, who seeks to harness spiritual achieve-ment to his own too human ends. The whole force of the Unborn, the Absolute, will crush him utterly.

What, then, is 'the ambit of my moral purpose' as Epictetus, the Stoic slave, described the basis of his teaching? I answer thus. THAT, which the Buddha called 'the Unborn, Unoriginated, Unformed' is in manifestation one. The Life-force in every form is one and undivided.

It follows that Wisdom can never be won by any man for himself alone. As a conduit pipe he applies all Wisdom gained in measureless compassion for all living things—and there is no thing dead. Wisdom/Compassion is a two-faced unity, the dual child of THAT. It follows reasonably, and the heart makes echo, that, as *The Voice of the Silence* puts it, 'the first step is to live to benefit mankind'. I believe this to be literally true and strive to live accordingly. Right Purpose, then, is for me the service of all life within the compass of my karmic fetters and opportunities.

Three Warnings

Now let us stand at the beginning, which for us is where and what we are, and survey the Road. Three warnings are here writ large for our inspection. Let us heed them. First, all progress will be by our own efforts. 'Work out your own salvation', said the Buddha, 'with diligence.' No scripture, book, or lecture, class or teacher will give us what we have not got, nor find for us what is already there. No Saviour will do a hand's turn on our behalf. We tread each yard of the Way on our own two feet, with guides to tell us of the Way ahead but with our own hands ever outstretched to help a younger brother along the weary, wind-swept path of self-development.

Next, the journey has taken and will take a very long time. Not in the next few years will a major pinnacle be reached with certainty, and it may not be for lives to come. Does it matter? The illusion of time is now our servant. As the Zen master Joshu said, 'People are used by twenty-four hours. I use twenty-four hours.' The second warning, therefore, is for patience. On this long journey there are no short cuts, neither of salvation by a Bodhisattva's Vow, nor lycergic acid, nor by the merriment of pseudo-Zen. I accept the doctrine of rebirth in its simple scriptural meaning, as a journey life after life on earth in each of which we continue 'day' by 'day' the lessons to be learnt, with periods of sleep between for rest and the digestion of experience. But as such I am patient of my own and my friends' development, and consider fifty years well spent in the conquest of one delusion, or a further glimpse or two of the Beyond of duality.

The third warning is equally clear, that though the Path leads to the end of suffering, the course of training here prescribed produces more, not less. This must be so, for the ego-self, now faced with death, is most unwilling to die, and as the self is transcended the pilgrim assumes the burden of others' woe, to an extent impossible to bear were it not for the growing joy of heart and mind which is born of the rhythm of entire becoming, and 'the Power divine which moves to good' which enters as the braggart self departs.

Needs for the Journey

What are the needs for the journey, beyond right motive? I *assume* a knowledge of Basic Buddhism, as I call it, for I still believe, as I wrote in *Zen, a Way of Life*, that Zen Buddhism has its roots in the Theravada, as expanded in the Mahayana and flowering in Zen. What more do we need? A high degree of thought-power, driving a highly-developed thinking mind. How can the limits of thought be broken and transcended unless the mind has reached the limits of thought? Zen is born where thinking ends; it is not a substitute. The same applies to will-power. Thought is a machine, consciousness using one of its faculties on one of its several planes, but it needs a powerful will to direct it unceasingly to the task in hand. As Dr Suzuki said, 'the will is the man and Zen appeals to it'. Zen, in plainer words, needs guts and lots of it. And finally we surely need some concept, dim though it be, of the Beyond, the Beyond of thinking, feeling, and all duality, beyond science and its horrid child, technology, which is not merely confined to the plane of duality in which we can only know *about* things, but is almost totally ignorant of five-sevenths of the planes on which humanity is born to function.

Gradual or Sudden

Will achievement be sudden or gradual? I cannot answer this perennial question for I fail to see the difference. *Of course* the years and lives of preparation are gradual, that is, step by step; *of course* each peep of the Absolute is sudden in that it happens in no-time. We walk into the sea, to the ankles, waist, chest; then suddenly we are swimming and the sea contains us. The clouds and earth on a sultry day become highly charged with positive and negative electricity. The build-up of force takes time but the discharge in a flash of lightning is sudden. Our eyes are shut; at last we open them and suddenly 'see'. Let us open them and see, not heaven but the world about us filled with, shining with, the very expression of, Zen.

Self-knowledge

I strongly advise the seeker of Zen to begin by acquiring knowledge about the complex entity in which 'he' or 'she' will discover Zen. The knowledge is all to hand and needs no text-books. Observe the physical body—be utterly physical as in a hot bath when you are tired and cold. Now lift your consciousness to the psychic plane, assuming you have the slightest knowledge of this vast field of consciousness. If you know nothing about it, learn, for it is the true seat of the senses, the source of illness, and the home of useful faculties such as telepathy. It is also the seat of 'hunches', not to be confused with intuitive, direct knowledge of the planes 'beyond'. And now the emotions, whatever they are. *Kama*, low desire, is, we are told, the source of suffering. Can we think without the defilement of craving, of hoping, fearing, desiring that things were other than they obviously are? Now concrete thought, as in business and home affairs. There is nothing physical, psychic or emotional in the creation of a shopping list, a balance sheet or a legal argument. But lift, if you can, to the plane of abstract thought, of general principles, cosmic laws, of the wider vision of wider minds, as philosophers, states-men or strenuous students of the inner life. These two-fold aspects of the mind are remarkably distinct, the low concerned with knowledge, argument, analysis and choice, the other with wisdom, the awareness of no-difference, of synthesis, of our ideals.

The Light of Intuition

Yet all these functions operate in the field of duality. To reach Zen we must climb to a higher point on the mountain, to a higher wave-band of Very High Frequency indeed—if we can. For at present few can reach this plane at will, and when we do tune in we seldom get an immediate reply. But at this stage begins a process which for me is the keynote of the road I tread—and strive to teach. If the process be not accepted as a possibility, or worth the attainment, I have nothing more to say. I call it irradiation, the sunlight of Buddhi, the intuition, breaking through. Buddhi seems to have two functions. On the one hand it is a built-in receiving set for the one Life-force of the Absolute, or the Dharmakaya, or the Unborn, the Void or, as any name is fatuous, THAT, as the Hindus call it. Thus do a million flowers each receive the sun, thus do electric lamps light up with a force which is not their own. But Buddhi then transmits this force, as much force as the instrument can take and digest—down into Manas, the mind. At least this happens to me and I need no other authority for its happening. And this is gradual and happens all the time as I study, meditate and wrestle with the inner principles of Life each moment of the day.

Then suddenly, yes, suddenly, come 'peeps' of a world we knew not of, of an everlasting Here, Now and doing This, which is 'nothing special' but enormously exciting, in which the 'suchness' of each thing is seen as every other thing, where form is obviously emptiness and emptiness is obviously form, where differences are no longer differences but aspects of totality, and Life in all its changing forms is one vast interrelated, rhythmic cycle of becoming, on the ceaseless round of birth, growth, decay and death, till the universe itself returns to the bosom of the Unborn whence it came. Can you not *see* this happening, here in London, at the bus stop, in the office and in bed?

Thus have I found and known, and along this line of training, which has worked for me and has worked in the last thirty-five years for many more, I propose to continue. All Buddhist schools teach mind-development; I call this character-training for it involves Sila, morality, as well as Bhavana, mind-development; and right motive, scarcely touched on in the Eightfold Path, which involves compassion as the peer of wisdom. Its nearest equivalent is Stoic philosophy, with the Buddhist concept of Dharma/Karma to determine and guide 'the ambit of one's moral purpose'. In some it leads to Zen.

Is this Training 'Cold'?
Some call this training 'cold'. I wonder what they mean. What is the opposite of 'too intellectual'? More emotional? May the gods (if such there be) forfend. Devotional, possibly, but what does this word mean in the minds of its London advocates? In some, I regret to notice, it means mere warmth of sloppy, comfortable feeling, with services in which the congregation do precisely nothing but feel 'warm'. Do they mean that the development of intellect is too hard work? Then show me the mystic in the world's history who had not clearly a first class mind. Do they want more 'heart', in the sense of compassion? None will move a foot along the way I advocate without it, for it is the basis of all that I teach and am. Do they want ritual? Then let them have it. Here is a way, or *dō*, as the Japanese call it, of great value. But it needs a powerful and controlled mind to operate it and a powerful will. If these notes portray a blend of Jnana and Karma Yoga, in Hindu terms, of course there are those on the way of Bhakti Yoga, the true way of Devotion. But this, as I understand that training, calls for a clear conception of the mystic's Goal, whether or not visualized in human form as the Beloved Master or as the far Ideal. And once again an intellect and a powerful will is needed. Let those, therefore, who find the Zen way, Rinzai, Soto or the above, too 'cold', walk parallel to these on the way of their own choosing.

The Need of Discipline
But the course I advocate needs discipline, self-discipline, for the right development of consciousness on all its planes in harmony. It involves

both study and meditation. By study I mean hard, intensive work on a book which rouses the intuition, whether a chosen scripture or the writings of men like the late Dr Suzuki; by meditation I mean subjective concentration on a given theme, preferably in a place apart with the minimum distraction. But how the pupil sits or whether he sits I care not; let him choose as the years go by the 'devices' which seem to bring the best results.

I have written enough, perhaps more than enough to describe what is done in my 'Zen Class'. If it be not Zen we will find another name for it if name be needed. Meanwhile we are busy. We have a job to do which is enormous fun and takes us precisely twenty-four hours a day. Let us get on with it.

10

A Note on Prajna, Dhyana and Samadhi

An understanding of these terms and the relationship between them is essential in one's study of Mahayana and especially Zen Buddhism. From Dr Suzuki's writings and lectures I therefore made the following notes for my own clarity of mind, and showed them to him in London. He made two small corrections but I understand that as they appear here he approved them.

Prajna, Wisdom, is the sudden, immediate awareness of the world of non-duality. It is beyond time, a touch of the Absolute. Satori is this awareness.

The word Prajna, in Chinese Chih Hui and in Japanese Chi Ye, is etymologically made up of Chi, perception or intelligence, and Ye, intuition; thus, intuitive perception.

Dhyana (Pali Jhana) is a form of meditation in time and duality. It is largely negative, as its object is to achieve a level-mindedness, or equilibrium or equanimity. It is a stilling of the waves of thought and emotion of everyday life. 'When the mind is disturbed the multiplicity of things is produced; when quieted, they disappear' (*Awakening of Faith*). Dhyana is the process of quietening. In this levelling the extremes of torpor and over-activity are alike overcome. The process of control is that described by Patanjali, Verse I, 'a hindrance of the modifications of the thinking principle'.

Dhyana leads to Samadhi, the highest of the four Jhanas or states of trance. Its gradual process leads to a state of consciousness which is as high as is possible short of actual Satori experience breaking through into the Absolute.

Etymologically the Chinese give two versions of the ideographs used for Samadhi, either to *hold equal*, as a balance, or as a smooth line as distinct from a violently wavy line, or else as *right acceptance*, receiving

96

things as they are. This means seeing them 'just so', or in their suchness, (*tathata*).

The sixth Patriarch, Hui-Neng, was the first to distinguish sharply Prajna from Dhyana, the former as sudden, indescribable, of the world of non-duality, and the latter as of duality, the goal of a process gradually achieved. Even at its highest Dhyana in Samadhi does not attain Prajna, though it may be good preparation for it.

But though Prajna and Dhyana are in one sense very different, belonging to the absolute and relative, non-dual and dual worlds respectively, they are not to be conceived separately. Prajna underlies and is the basis of Dhyana, and makes it possible, and without Prajna there could be no Dhyana. They are two modes of what should be one awareness.

If we visualize Samadhi as a level line (with the rapid fluctuations of normal consciousness quieted), the 'moment' of Satori will cut it at right angles from below. In our thinking we visualize a sequence of a, b, c, d, etc., but this is born of our illusion. While looking at a or b we cut off the essential flow of life and then label that part of the line as a or b. There is no such separation, only an unbroken continuum. But the sequence, however far stretched, never achieves infinity. Where, then, do we find infinity? It must be here and now, in the sequence itself. From the 'deeps' of the (absolute) unconscious comes the sudden flash of Satori, which *must* be sudden, a jump, however long the preparation for it, and that moment of the flash is seen as eternity. That thing or moment is timeless and absolute, and though in one sense it is a part of the whole it is in fact the whole. Thus any one thing, seen in Satori, is all other things, including its opposite (*jijimuge*). In that 'moment' all things are seen when any one thing is seen for what it is, in its suchness, and as void.

Thus preparation for enlightenment is necessary and necessarily gradual, but the moment when it comes is sudden, a leap from the relative duality to the absolute non-duality. Though Samadhi be attained through Dhyana, and last for hours on end, it is not Satori. Satori may come at any time, in Samadhi or while digging in the garden, as described by many stories from Zen monasteries. What matters is the intensity of will; the 'moment' will come when it comes.

G

THE COURSE

11

A Western Approach to Zen

Buddhism is a Western term for the great body of doctrine, tradition and culture that stems from the enlightenment of Gautama the Buddha. Various schools arose among his followers, including the Theravada, whose canon in Pali began to be written down in the first century BC; and the two schools of the Mahayana, the Madyamika, associated with the name of Nagarjuna, and the Mind-Only school founded centuries later by Asanga and Vasubandhu.

In due course the teaching of the Buddha, in one form or another, flowed along the old silk road to China. The Chinese reception to the Message, which arrived in the first century AD, was cool. Here are monks, the Chinese complained, who do no work to earn their living, have no sons to honour the memory of their parents, and are bound by a large number of rules quite inappropriate to the climate of China.

About AD 500, Bodhidharma, an Indian Buddhist with most unorthodox views and methods of teaching, arrived at the Chinese Court, and was granted audience with the Emperor. The traditional account of the interview makes it unique in the history of religion.

The Emperor boasted of all he had done to further the cause of Buddhism. He went into detail and asked at the end, 'Now what is my merit?' 'None whatsoever', replied his visitor. The Emperor tried again. 'What is the First Principle of Buddhism?' 'Vast Emptiness,' said Bodhidharma, 'and nothing holy therein.' 'Who, then, now confronts me?' asked the Emperor. 'I have no idea', said Bodhidharma.

The Chinese loved this, although they may not have observed its profundity, and in due course there was born the Ch'an school, which has been described as the Chinese reaction to Indian Buddhism. Further Patriarchs followed Bodhidharma but it was the sixth, Hui-Neng, who turned a new tradition of teaching into an organized school. For five hundred years there was a succession of great teachers until, about AD 1200, Ch'an Buddhism arrived in Japan as Zen, where a parallel development took place of the Rinzai and Soto schools.

The essence of Hui-Neng's teaching is clear. It is that of the 'Wisdom that has gone beyond' (Prajnaparamita) of the Madhyamika school as applied directly and without compromise to daily life. Long hours of meditation have their value, but in themselves will no more lead to enlightenment than polishing a brick will turn it into a mirror. There must be the sudden opening of the 'third eye' of Prajna-intuition to see, as Hui-Neng proclaimed, that 'from the first not a thing is', that 'all distinctions are falsely imagined', that 'in Buddhism there are no two things'. This return to the direct teaching of the Buddha himself was complemented by the later master Huang Po, who taught that 'all sentient beings are nothing but the One Mind, beside which nothing exists'.

Thus in the crucible of direct experience the Ch'an masters fused the teachings of the two great schools of the Mahayana, and applied their wisdom to work in the fields, the market and the home.

Stories about these masters were collected and handed down, as also specimens of the *mondo* or rapid question/answer by which the master would attempt to help the pupil break out of the fetters of his thinking. But whereas the early masters taught their pupils face to face according to their need, later masters began to rely on the koan, of which the first on record is that of Hui-Neng himself, who persuaded the robbers pursuing him to sit in silence for a while, after which he asked them, 'When you are thinking neither of good nor evil, what is at that moment your original face [or essence of Mind]?' These enigmatic sayings or questions, without obvious sense, are used to break the mould of thought and to release the mind 'to abide nowhere'.

Hundreds of koans were in time produced, such as 'what is the sound of one hand clapping?', and even classified, and for the last fifteen hundred years the training in Rinzai Zen Buddhism has been based upon them. But whereas this is evidence that the system works for a Japanese monk in a monastery, it is poor evidence that it would be right for a Western mind in daily life. In my experience the koan system should not be used in the absence of a qualified teacher, for it involves the production of increasing pressure in the mind of the pupil who is driven, as it were, down a blind alley with a brick wall at the end of it. If a competent master is watching the final stages, ready, as it is said, to help the chicken break out of the egg and, equally important, ready to approve the resulting 'experience' and to help with the long process of 'maturing' it, the method may succeed for the few. But in the absence of such a master the pressure may actually break the mind concerned and produce not enlightenment but insanity.

Then what is left for Europe? Zen training in Japan involves long days and years of deep meditation, whether on the given koan or, as is more usual in Soto Zen, just 'sitting', and this assumes a monastic life and almost unlimited time. Nowadays a few go to Japan from the West, learn Japanese and submit themselves to the training, but so far none has returned to Europe with approved enlightenment. Conversely, Rinzai masters have visited Europe, occasionally for months on end, and accepted pupils for the duration of the visit. These visits have not been a success if only because the time available was quite inadequate. I therefore take the view, expressed these last ten years, that the hundreds of Western Buddhists genuinely interested in Zen Buddhism must find an alternative to the traditional training of Japan. Here are four reasons for this grave decision.

1. It is unreasonable to expect Europeans in the 1970s to adopt a system of spiritual training formulated for the Chinese in AD 700.

2. If it *were* right for Europe, it would need a large body of qualified Japanese teachers, between them speaking many languages and prepared to give long years to training those students who wished to become their pupils. Conversely, the training would be confined to the few Westerners with the time and money for a long visit to Japan.

3. The faculty by which, in Buddhist terms, the West is working out its Dharma is the intellect, a superb instrument for the acquisition of truth in the field of duality. In my view it cannot be by-passed or ignored. It must be developed and used to the full before the Western consciousness can, by developing the intuition, transcend its inherent limitations and achieve a direct vision of Reality. Only by reaching the end of thought shall we break through to the beyond of thought, which is Prajna-intuition, the 'third eye' with which alone we shall perceive and know that we already are enlightened.

4. We in the West are householders, and monastic life is no longer normal save for the few. We have a part to play in the total life of the community. While using meditation as a planned part of the daily life we must find an approach to Zen awareness which uses the day's adventure to that end.

Much of the intellectual background of Zen Buddhism is now available in English. Thanks to the work of Dr Edward Conze, we have much of 'the Wisdom that has gone Beyond', and we have some twenty books of the scriptures of Zen Buddhism, its meaning and practice, from the late Dr D. T. Suzuki, who gave his life to making known as much as words may tell of this, perhaps the most truly Buddhist school of Buddhism. But it is not enough to arouse interest and provide the intellectual background. There must be a definite method of self-training aimed at a break-through to the 'Unborn, Unoriginated, Unformed'. What is it to be? That is the problem, and it is not new. I drew attention to it in 1960 in a book called *Zen Comes West*, and I have so far heard no answer other than my own.

It involves a long course of mind-training, parallel with those of the Theravada and the various traditions of Tibet. It needs some preliminary mind development acquired in this life or in lives gone by; the will-power necessary to carry through any training once begun, however strange and seeming difficult, and common sense in application.

But here is a crisis, not to be lightly ignored. As Hui-Neng and his successors point out, with all the force at their command, it is impossible to enlighten the mind, for the mind, as an inseverable part of All-Mind or Buddha-Mind, is already enlightened. As Hui-Neng, with a thunder voice proclaimed, 'From the first not a thing is, 'and this is the heart of the Prajnaparamita philosophy, which is the highest that Buddhism or any other philosophy-religion has attained. Or, in the words of Huang Po again, 'All sentient beings are nothing but the One Mind, beside which nothing exists'. It seems to follow that, viewed on its own plane, the enormous complex of thought, feeling, will and desire that we call mind can never *become* the Buddha-Mind, for it is attachment to its product, thought, which alone prevents us seeing that we are in essence already Buddha-Mind, which includes both Nirvana and Samsara, the Absolute of Non-duality and the relativity of daily life. To work on this mind is therefore more than unnecessary, worse than useless; it is pernicious, in that it may but pander to a subtly inflated ego.

How, then, shall we dare to do this very thing, to work on the present mind with a view to seeing that we are, and have been all the time, enlightened? How shall we dare to train this individual mind which, on the plane of Buddha-Mind, does not even exist? I answer boldly, because the difference between mind and Buddha-Mind is, like all distinctions, in the words of Hui-Neng 'falsely imagined'. We are mind as much as we are Buddha-Mind, and the course that I suggest destroys this false antithesis, as equally that of self and Self, or the flame and the Light. Surely the whole man climbs to the summit, 'muddy boots and all', taking all things with him, good and evil, truth and lies, to re-become the Essence of Mind which never ceased to be his own divinity.

When, therefore, the masters of Zen appeal to us 'to drop it', meaning mind and all to do with it, or emphasize that 'all duality is falsely imagined', surely we have here such a false antithesis? Should we not use the mind we have and largely are to achieve reunion with its source? But I agree that the distinction must be *seen* to be false, not merely with a thought, however illumined, but with the light of intuition as im-mediate, direct awareness, a break-through to Reality.

But HOW? How does the average, dedicated Western seeker after Life and its own high purpose begin to lift his consciousness to the plane where all these splendid sayings are true? The Buddha gave an answer, that of the Noble Eightfold Path, which includes right purpose largely bereft of selfishness, right action in the world of men, and then right training of the mind to the level of Samadhi, the sweet calm of perfect mind-control. Did all the Zen masters find a by-pass round this clearly defined, hard Way? Or are they speaking from the level of achieved attainment when, illusion shed, they see from the height of a Buddha-Mind that they have never ceased to be? If so, how did they get there?

Surely there must be analysis before synthesis, examination of the illusion we must learn to see as such, awareness of infinite difference before a realization that the Many never cease to be One.

Even if the purpose of Zen training is to see that there is nothing to attain, whence this seeing, save by examination, with the highest mind we can command, of the nature of Samsara, which we are told we shall one day know to be Nirvana in its earthly guise? And this involves the training and right use of the mind.

I suggest that what is needed by the Western student, and was once in some form used by all who now speak from the plane of Prajna-intuition, is a flight of steps up which we *gradually* climb the 'hundred-foot pole', from the top of which we jump, with an existential leap, into *sudden* Zen awareness.

The steps here suggested, all of which are within the ambit of the seventh and eighth of the Noble Eightfold Path, have the merit of being reasonable, suited to the Western mind and temperament, safe in the absence of a qualified teacher for much at least of the climb, and above all they work! Slowly, steadily, safely we raise consciousness until, progressively illumined by the growing light of enlightenment, we are ready for the first 'peeps' of the new awareness, and meanwhile serve with humble, dedicated heart the needs of all mankind.

This is no place to set out the course of long self-training which, from raw experience in my own life and in the Zen Class of the Buddhist Society, I offer to the Western seeker after Zen.

I can but summarize the notes included for each Phase which, over the period of months allocated, are expanded, discussed and used as the basis for consistent meditation.

Phase One. 'Unthink'

Before thought can be transcended we must examine the nature of thought, the thought process and the extent to which our minds are now conditioned by past thinking, present thought-habits and habitual reaction to stimulus.

Before we can build 'the hundred foot tower' from which to take 'an existential leap' into the enlightenment-experience we must largely clear the foundations of outworn thought and now unneeded thinking.

Only then shall we be able to practise genuine thought-control, the quieting down of the waves of thought, and reach 'the still centre of the turning world', the Buddha-Mind within.

First, then, let us look at our present general and particular conditioning, and make some attempt at 'de-conditioning' to break our bondage and to clear up the resulting mess.

At the close of each phase we ask ourselves searching questions. Here we ask, 'How much am I still bound to particular views on religion, politics, social problems? Can I honestly see the other man's point of view on anything in issue, anything at all? And finally, can I visualize, however dimly, a Truth which is above and beyond both of any pair of opposites, which *was* before the difference was born?'

Phase Two. 'Stop Thinking'

Having faced the mind's conditioning, and begun to detach it from outworn thoughts and undesirable thought-habits, we must go further.

We shall not in fact stop thinking for there is no need, but we must learn to decide what we think, and when and why, and to turn off the tap when finished. The same will apply to controlling our reaction to outside stimulus or to invading thoughts from within.

The all but impossible ideal is to 'let the mind abide nowhere' or, in the words of the Heart Sutra, 'to dwell without thought-coverings'. We are yet far from it. Let us move just that much nearer.

After months of this we shall ask ourselves questions, such as, 'Can I now for minutes on end stop all reaction to outside events or objects, not in deep meditation but as I move around? Can I cease at will from 'mental chattering'? In particular, can I stop approving or disapproving of what others do or say? Can I really mind my own business? Have I the moral strength to refuse to form an opinion about happenings around me or at large? Can I frankly change an opinion once formed?'

Up to this point we are pupils back at school, with a list of books for study, loose-leaf notebooks and a compulsory period each day for study and/or meditation as found needful. The theme being used at the time is held at the back of the mind all day, to come forward into consciousness at every moment when the mind is free to work on it. The pupil is not yet concerned with Zen experience or anything to do with 'Zen'.

Concentration and Meditation. The clear distinction between these two employments of the mind should be thoroughly understood. Western Buddhists today are much concerned with meditation but the practice is entangled with too much technical jargon. Meditation is not natural to the mind and should if practised remain as simple as possible. Surely it is sufficient to learn to concentrate and then, when opportunity permits, to turn a searchlight into the mind in search of Buddha-Mind. Such at least is the belief of many.

Phase Three. '*Re-think*'
Now for the first time the mind is lifted as high as may be into the realm of intuitive awareness. What is Zen? Alas, 'the Tao [or Zen or Truth] that can be named [described] is not the eternal Tao' [or Zen or Truth]. Zen is not a thing, not an idea nor yet a noble ideal. Nor can it be attained for we live already in its abiding place, Pure-Mind.

> *One day we shall find that all thought stands in the way of our enlighten-ment. Not yet. We must now deliberately use great thought to raise consciousness to the threshold of a new faculty, the intuition. This will increasingly illumine thinking until the first brief moments come of direct, im-mediate vision of things as they are, beyond duality of thought or feeling. These great thought-forces must be invited, deeply studied and allowed to remould the total man. There will be conflict, for the price of victory is the death of self.*

Here is the heart of the system of self-training which I have used for fifty years and humbly advocate. Let but one of these vast 'Thought-forces' enter the mind *at its own level*, or as near as may be, and the total man is re-created. This is a claim which argument cannot effect; it will be found to be true or not. There is here no fear of an uncontrolled irruption from the unconscious; these thoughts are welcome guests, flames of the Light, as a light switched on to dispel the deep gloom of illusion. To use them is to remove all fear of the manifold forms of pseudo-Zen, the snatching of unlawful moments of a false awareness by selfish pressure to attain. These trance conditions and forced glimpses of the psychic plane are as different from the 'no-moment' of true Satori as pewter from pure gold, deceiving no one but the fool who waits to be deceived. There are no short cuts to Enlightenment.

These cosmic principles are difficult to imprison in a phrase, for though each was once a shrine for a vast experience, the words have largely lost their meaning and become the debased coinage of third-rate literature. 'Life is One' is a fair example, tremendous in its implications, from the brotherhood of man to the fact that there is no death, save of an outworn form. 'From the first not a thing is' said Hui-Neng. Can our present mind conceive, and use, such pure idealism? It can try. That Prajna, Wisdom, and Karuna, Compassion are one inseverable unity is, according to Dr Suzuki, the basis of Mahayana. Here the Arhat and the Bodhisattva doctrines are seen to be indivisible, and the Bodhisattva doctrine is, I believe, fast gaining ground in the field of Western thought. Again, Karma is much more than the drear equation of cause-effect, it is rather a sweeping vision of the Universe as total Harmony, which broken, the breaker first and then all manifestation must restore. Thus Karma is seen as the regulator of the Unborn/Born relation and of the least part of it. And finally, in this choice from dozens such, 'It's all right' or, as a Zen master put it, 'the snowflakes fall, each in its proper place'. Or in the words already cited of poet Thoreau, 'I know that the enterprise is worthy. I know that things work well. I have heard no bad news.'

As these forces surge and thunder through the mind, smashing the barriers of outworn thought, dissolving the ego, washing away distinctions, limitations and choices grimly held, consciousness is raised just that much nearer to the level of its own true home, 'the Essence of Mind' which is, as Hui-Neng put it, 'intrinsically pure'. Here is the field of what I call Illumined Thought, great thinking lit with increasing certainty as the light of the intuition proves or disproves the concepts dwelling in the mind.

Such a condition is visible to all, for all 'great' minds, so-called by their fellows, are expanded and illumined minds, illumined one would say with the Buddha-light of Prajna-intuition, the 'third Eye' opened to see things as they are. Many such minds are clearly often more than so illumined; they have achieved some measure of Satori. Many of the finest philosophers, astronomers, scientists, poets, statesmen, ecclesiastics, men of commerce and of war, have spoken of experience which can be fairly so described. And there is here no limiting claim for Buddhist influence. It is of interest that several of the few already known to us whose 'break-through' has the marks of authenticity had never heard of Buddhism, still less of Zen.

Meanwhile the student, secure in illumined thought, looks for a bridge from duality to Non-duality, from the unreal to the Real. In truth there is none and there can be none, yet the bridge is crossed, the journey made, and safely now. Knowledge, become wisdom, flowers in compassion. Possessed of sound character, moved with true motive, safe from the 'ballooning' of the ego and the seduction of short-cuts, the climber climbs with skilful mountaineering. Each 'peep' of Reality is a solid gain. There is *gradual* progress of the total man to *sudden* bright experience. In due course, 'when the pupil is ready the master appears'. We shall have earned him.

Phase Four. Beyond Thought

> As the ceiling of Samsara, the dual world of unreality, is pierced with the sword of Prajna-intuition, allowing 'peeps' of a wider state of consciousness, we reach the true beginning of Zen training. Each experience is incommunicable in words but each has the common factor that self has disappeared. These are 'moments of awareness', not of my awareness of any thing which was not there before. Here subject/object, past, present and future, you and I no longer exist in separation. We now see everything as it is, and all things as inseverable parts of the same Fullness/Emptiness. This is the true beginning of Zen training which Dr Suzuki called 'a moral training based on the experience of Satori'. Let us walk on!

The Teacher Can But Point the Way

'O Master, I am sick and sad.
Teach me what I should know.'

'My child, there is No Thing above,
No thing to teach below.'

'Master, I suffer. Be my guide;
Surely the Way is clear.
Show me the steps that I may tread
To freedom, now and here.'

'My child, if I may do no less
I yet can do no more.
For each alone shall find the stream
And gain the further shore.
The steps are many. First, to look
To see things as they are.
Accepting each as truly such,
A dewdrop or a star.
Then know that each is all of each,
Of heaven or earth or hell.
All good is evil, evil good,
And all, my child, is well!'

'To walk unceasingly is hard;
Still harder to begin!'

'Yet strive to reach with heart and mind
The vision seen within.
The self you love is but a mist
Exuded by the mind
To blur the heart's compassion
For all life and all mankind.

The Self, the light that has no name,
Is mirror to the Void.
It is. We have and have it not,
Alloyed and unalloyed.
And now walk on. I do not lead.
We travel side by side
Until the heart is love itself,
And love itself has died.'

'Master, your finger points the Way;
Your wisdom is my friend.
But when the long hard journey's done?'

'My child, there is no end.'

12

Phase One: 'Unthink'

If Zen be described for our purpose as the opening of the 'third' eye' of Wisdom-intuition, and such awakening be regarded as the source and goal of all Zen training, how do we raise consciousness to the plane or level or wave-length of this intuition? Do we just sit and hope, or do we move with planned deliberation to such a 'consummation devoutly to be wished'?

The answer is clear but must be emphasized. We wish to see a pregnant term in Zen. None hinders us from seeing but each must remove the bandages from his own eyes. As the Dhammapada puts it, 'even Buddhas do but point the Way', or, in Western terms, as formulated by Plotinus, 'Out of discussion we call to vision, to those desiring to see we point the path; our teaching is a guiding in the way; the seeing must be the very act of him who has made the choice.' Or again, as an English Bhikkhu said long ago, 'the Buddha gives you a ticket but you must take the train!'

If Zen is beyond thought, as all agree, we must each free ourselves from the bonds of thought and present thinking. We must be master where at present we are slave. Ar Dr Suzuki wrote, 'What distinguishes Zen from other spiritual teachings is its perfect mastery over words or concepts. Instead of becoming a slave to them, it is aware of the role they play in human experience, and assigns them to the place to which they properly belong.' The thought-machine must be brought under control, in order that it may be rightly used to raise consciousness to its limits, and beyond. The operative word is control. Look once more at the ideal, 'to let the mind abide nowhere', to use it as a bird flying free, as a car which is never stuck to the road it uses.

We do not achieve this condition with a splendid gesture, but with years and lives of very hard work. Zen speaks of a hundred-foot pole up which we climb—and jump, with an existential leap into enlightenment, a state of mindlessness, no-thought. I suggest a humbler analogy, a pair of steps, high steps and many of them, steps which may be numbered and one by one achieved. But even this humble form of erection must be soundly based or it will fall, we with it. To build a house the wise man clears the ground and digs to sound foundations. This ground has a double meaning, as in the analogy and as the 'ground' of spiritual wisdom, the common basis of all true experience. And the higher the building the deeper the foundations, and we are building very high.

Surely it follows that to master the vast process of thought, to erect a temple of intellectual understanding from the top of which we 'see' as never before, we must first clear the site. Upon it now, as we shall soon be forced to admit, is a hideous collection of derelict, abandoned and forgotten buildings on which no sane man would attempt to build a temple, or even a meditation cell. In the same way, on a cleared site there must be foundations equal to the building planned. In terms of mind we shall need to dig into the unconscious, into which so much of our abandoned thinking/feeling has been deeply pressed. Thus the task before us in Phase One is harder than at first imagined.

But surely this process of clearing and digging must come first in our own self-training. Anyone who has lectured to an audience on ideas strange to them knows the sensation of throwing pebbles at an iron wall. The thoughts, though admitted to be 'interesting', just bounce off and fall, as most of the seed in Jesus' parable of the sower, on stony ground. The soil was not only unprepared but was rock-like in its resistance to new ideas. How, then, in our own minds can we plant new seed, even of Buddhist basic principles, without regard to the state of the mind in which we are sowing them?

So let us examine our present minds, a dreary, tiresome and exhausting task, but needful indeed. Look at your mind, quietly and with pencil and paper in hand. Consider its conditioning. Hui-Neng says 'the Essence of Mind is intrinsically pure'. It may be so, but it has a vast collection of rubbish piled up round it! As a Japanese professor wrote recently, 'the trouble human beings have about learning anything does not as a rule arise from the intrinsic difficulty of the lessons to be learned, but rather from the fact that before any new notions can be grasped we have so much to unlearn, our cherished sentimentalities, our inherited dogmas, our superstitions, our pet intellectual clichés— all serving to nullify, distort or caricature beyond recognition the lessons we receive'. The situation is worse than that. Make a list, an actual list of fifty of your present beliefs, conclusions, working principles of morality and social behaviour. Go on with religious convictions, irrevocable choices, formulated ambitions, political opinions and far ideals. How many of these are now outworn and pushed into the lumber-room, or joined in fatuous conjunction with later thoughts at variance? These are undesirable; far worse are thoughts still living, which pull one hither and yon without our noticing. These are living bonds, adhesions limiting the movement of a joint, anchors which nullify the noblest aspirations of our sails. Note further still, our present automatic reaction to all stimuli, the further fetters being daily made.

All these are hard indeed to break or even to stretch. I copied the following from *Punch*: 'It is possible to get rid of a mosquito, a battle-ship or even a woman. The one thing ineradicable, the thing that a man's life is not enough to eliminate, is a preconceived idea.' Only a strong mind can face the fact of this conditioning; a very strong mind is needed utterly to break it. What is the incentive to begin and carry on this lifelong task? May I quote an answer from a modern Roshi, the late Sokei-an Sasaki. 'When a Zen teacher says, "Go back to your original state" (the "intrinsically Pure Mind" of Hui-Neng) he asks you to root from your mind all thoughts and the many names of many things. He asks you to get rid of all padding, to clear away all debris, to make your mind pure as pure water. This is the mind's original state.'

This is the point to be ever born in mind. In the words of Hui-Neng, 'the Essence of Mind is intrinsically pure.' How do we reach this purity, we who in fact are already pure? It is all very well to say, 'by clearing away the debris in the mind to make it clear as water'. But how?

Just see how gravely bound you are, for the very seeing will be a step towards the fetters' loosening. Ask yourself, are you truly willing to see the other side in an argument, even to change sides, and to express, for the benefit say of an absent friend, the other point of view? *Must* you form an opinion on matters of no concern of yours, and voice them firmly, knowing that your knowledge of the subject is extremely limited? Can you sit on the fence above all argument and even visualize the 'higher Third' of every pair of opposites? If so you are rather remarkable; if not you are bound indeed. Yet this deplorable mess of mind is one of the five constituents of the personality according to Buddhist teaching, your karmic deposit leading to your next rebirth.

Let us face it; we are all conditioned biologically and by our animal instincts; by our race, colour, caste, sex and religious upbringing; by our family, education, environment and job. All these have gone to form and still affect our choosing, views, opinions, and our reaction to outside stimulus. The resultant mind is thereby bound by a mass of thought-forms, old, new and habitual, of loves and hates, fashions, phobias, conclusions and ideals. And each of us is further bound by his psychological type and racial and personal unconscious. What a long way is this from 'Let the mind abide nowhere'! For we have chosen, or had chosen for us, our views on politics, classical or modern art, and quite unchangeable opinions on the behaviour of some government somewhere in its behaviour towards somebody else somewhere else. Yet we talk of an approach to Zen!

With these and more the mind is overfull. A Zen master asked a visitor whose mind was full of learning, 'Would you like some tea?' He went on pouring until the cup overflowed on the mat. The visitor protested. 'But how can I give you tea', asked the master, 'unless you first empty your overfull cup?'

Of all these entanglements perhaps the habit of choice, often irrevocable, is the most limiting, for Zen consciousness implies, above all, liberation from choice. As we read in 'On Trust in the Heart',

> To set up what you like against what you dislike
> This is the disease of the mind.
> Try not to seek after the true:
> Only cease to cherish opinions.

Relativity implies duality. In the world of Samsara we are faced with a hundred choices a day and make them all. But each binds. We have clung to this or that bank of the river but life flows down between them, and we have stopped on the way. The Buddhist ideal is the Middle Way, and the least move to either side of its middle necessitates a return to the middle, probably at the expense of a swing of the pendulum too far the other way.

What are these fetters, and how did they appear? All thought is a process of division, and every thought, idea, belief is of necessity partial, and therefore of necessity partly wrong. Thoughts must be used for communication and for intellectual understanding, but as Huang Po says, 'Why seek a doctrine? As soon as you have a doctrine you fall into dualistic thought.' Hence seeking for the truth can never satisfy. 'Your seeking', Huang Po said to his enquirer, 'makes a difference between (in this case) past and present. If you were to stop seeking how could there be any difference between them?'

Yet seek we must, and use the tool of thought in the process. But as we do so let us bear in mind the famous first verse of the Dhammapada; 'All that we are is the product of our thoughts. . . .' We are what we have made ourselves, or good or bad as we regard the product, for 'there is nothing good or bad but thinking makes it so'.

We must think, then, and deliberately, and thought as such is right. Our error is in being bound by it. It is the attachment to thought that holds us back from Zen Enlightenment, and we are at present sadly bound.

But even if every thought is a prison, at least let us modify the danger by the constant use of doubt. Let us be humble and not quite so sure of any belief, decision or conclusion. As Professor Tucci, the authority on Tibetan Buddhism, put it, 'Avoid the harshness of unyielding certainty'. Let us watch the birth of a thought or feeling and slay most of them at birth. Let us use them, as a man uses a raft to cross a river; thereafter he leaves the raft behind. As Hui-Neng says, 'Our mind should stand aloof from circumstances, and on no account should we allow them to influence the functioning of our mind'. Alas, we allow each word we read or see, each word we hear to influence our circumstances. We are not flying free. How shall we free ourselves? Let us look again at our own list of anchors, fetters, adhesions and all other manner of mental bondage.

There are views which we should totally abandon and if possible root out of the mind. There are views which we may provisionally hold and use because for a while at least they are useful. And there are what I call thought-forces, to be introduced in Phase Three, and deliberately used to raise consciousness to the beyond of thought.

In the Zen Class of the Buddhist Society, for which this course was fashioned, we suggest examples of these general lists and make observations about them. Here there is little room for examples, but two at least of the first type may be mentioned. We must root out every trace of the concept of authority. Do we still look to God, or some such figure as a Force to save us from our sins and their unpleasant consequences? Or have we some lesser authority, alive or dead, in being or as a projected image of a virtue yet unwon? Are we still guru-hunting, regarding the writings of A or B as authority for any statement made therein? If so remember the Buddha's own advice to the Kalamas. You will find it in any of a hundred books on Buddhism. More stringent still is the saying, 'Do not follow in the footsteps of the ancient ones. Seek what they sought!' And a second thought to be rooted out is the doctrine, a dangerous half-truth, that each man has an immortal soul. All schools of Buddhism utterly eschew belief in an unchanging self of any kind in man. The Atman of Hindu philosophy is no man's possession, but a reflection of THAT, which the Buddha called the

'Unborn, Unoriginated, Unformed'. This Unborn manifests in Samsara as one indivisible Life-Force whose countless forms are interdependent, interrelated and karmically one. 'All distinctions are falsely imagined', said Hui-Neng, and the belief in my soul, my mind, my will as something separate from yours is illusion. True, there is in every man a 'soul' in the sense of a bundle of attributes or character which moves from life to life on the long road to enlightenment, but as Dr McGovern put it in his *Introduction to Mahayana Buddhism*, 'Buddhism insists that the soul is not a rigid, unchanging, self-constituted entity but a living, complex, changing, evolving organism'. Digest this well, for how can the mind of man fly free, alighting nowhere, if it seriously believes in a personal immortal soul?

Alas, there are many more such thoughts still strongly held or only partially discarded. As for the second category, those ideas which are, so to speak, the working tools of our daily life, let us use them fully, always remembering that he is a fool who is permanently stuck to his spade, his typewriter or his car.

We need a reasonable quantum of 'Buddhist principles', for our own application and to offer our friends. Of such are the basic teachings of Theravada Buddhism as modified, expanded and enriched by Mahayana developments. Let us study and daily use the Three Signs of Being, the Four Noble Truths, Karma and Rebirth and the concept of Nirvana. Let us add to these the Bodhisattva ideal of the Mahayana, compassion coeval with wisdom, the Beyond of thought and the direct, immediate path to it of Zen. But even here we must be vulnerable to alien thought. We must be ready to modify or even abandon any of them, be tolerant of those who scorn them, examine our own belief from time to time. The ideal is to be naked to experience, to 'dwell without thought-coverings', as advised in the Heart Sutra. 'We must try to get life itself', says Dr Suzuki, 'instead of thinking about it, but thinking is needed to reach that ultimate point of living.' After all, Buddhism, Enlightenment and many more ideas are still for us but words, the outer covering of concepts. But 'Teachings point to the Goal, they do not contain it'. Let us use such thoughts but not get stuck to them.

It has been greatly said that 'Buddhism is the way of becoming the Buddha'. The paramount need for every student is direct experience and we must all of us look deeply into Buddhist principles to see if for us, here, now, they are true. All are man-made, as principles and in their wording. All are so much partial understanding of the Wisdom of the Buddha-Mind in each of us. Even the Buddha's experience could never be totally enshrined in words. His teaching came out of his experience and to understand it we must go to the source of it, the same experience.

Let us, then, examine each his mind; destroy at least adhesions to a vast array of thoughts and use but lightly those we find to be helpful on the Way.

In the Zen Class we end by asking ourselves such questions as the following, and demanding truthful answers:

1. *How fully am I still conditioned mentally? How deeply am I still attached to one or other of a hundred opinions and points of view?*

2. *How much am I still bound by my upbringing to particular views on religion, politics, social problems?*

3. *How much am I still bound by my mental make-up, extrovert or introvert, intellectual type or man of action, in a body male or female, old or young?*

4. *Can I with effort honestly see the other man's point of view on anything in issue, anything at all?*

5. *Can I visualize, however dimly, a Truth which is above and beyond both of any pairs of opposites, which was before the difference was born?*

13

Buddhism and God

In Phase One we spoke of concepts, beliefs and conclusions which bind the mind, and make nonsense of the ideal, to 'let the mind abide nowhere'. One such is the reliance on 'authority'.

In Phase Two we shall speak of mind-control, which is ability to think as we please and not otherwise. This again implies a freedom from outside restraint, a power of choice in all reaction to stimulus. But this in turn implies the absence of any sense of authority, and the supreme symbol of such for many students is still the concept of God. Let us therefore examine this particular fetter in some detail, as an example of a hundred more.

We in the West are steeped in the concept of God. We are most of us brought up in a Christian atmosphere, and taught at an impressionable age the story of Jesus and the teachings of Christianity. The latter are based on the concept of a god who is at the same time Absolute yet personal, the omnipotent Creator of the Universe who yet answers the most personal needs of the least of his creatures. As children we may have been puzzled at the muddled emotions which bind mankind to this supreme Being, how he loves while he punishes, should be feared while he is loved, is all good while permitting evil and, while standing as the Creator of all things, is only concerned with a small proportion of the inhabitants of this tiny planet. This ambivalence of emotion, as some of us later discovered, is the result of projecting into the sky a God whose parts and principles reflect some of the worst as well as the best ingredients of the near-Eastern mind. As a wit remarked, 'In the beginning God made man in his own image, and man has been returning the compliment ever since'.

But it is far easier to analyse this view of God and then to reject it from the conscious mind than to extract it without leaving roots from what Jung calls the personal unconscious. As a metaphysical concept, such as a theory of cosmic causation, or the ultimate relation of the parts and the whole, it can do no damage, and may not even affect the mind. As Jung says, in *The Secret of the Golden Flower*, 'If I accept the fact that a god is absolute and beyond all human experience, he leaves me cold. But if I know, on the other hand, that God is a mighty activity in my soul, at once I must concern myself with him; he can then become even unpleasantly important. . . .' The distinction is profound, for we cannot 'understand' these first beginnings or final ends. We may learn more and more *about* them; we never know them. These are indeed the matters which it profits not a man to argue or discuss, and about them the Buddha ever maintained a 'noble silence'. God as a product of thinking is therefore a harmless inhabitant of our spiritual sky, for he is at best a creation of our mind, and bears no relation to the Reality that thought can neither contact nor describe. But God as a psychological fact, as a 'mighty activity' in the mind is as real as anything else in a world of relative reality. And God in this sense is not a 'thing' that we may drop from the mind at will. Before it can be removed the process of projection which gave it life must be slowly reversed until the courageous thinker is faced with his own 'shadow' and has, as it were, consumed it.

This needs great courage, for we all love to blame others for our own shortcomings. If I may quote again from Jung, who in this field is the greatest mind in Europe, 'Such a man lives in the "house of self-collection". Such a man knows that whatever is wrong in the world is in himself, and if he only learns to deal with his own shadow he has done something real for the world. He has succeeded in removing an infinitesimal part at least of the unsolved, gigantic social problems of our day. . . .' From the Buddhist point of view he has done more. In learning to become 'mindful and self-possessed' he is learning to 'work out his own salvation, with diligence'. But if the wise man should cease to project his own 'shadow', the dark side of his soul, on to his surroundings and his fellow men, he must also learn to withdraw the existing projection of his spiritual needs from the muddled concept of a painfully human God. The later stages of this process are the harder, for it is a paradoxical truth that the closer the projection the harder it is to see it as such and so to analyse and remove it. We see the folly of worshipping a tribal God on religious and national occasions; it is much more difficult to see as projected gods our loved ideals or dreaded phobias. If our God has shrunk to that soulless entity, 'the State', it is no less a projection of our personal insufficiency; when smaller still, as 'the Department', beloved of the official mind, or some new 'ism' or vaguely as the Needs of the People, or even Science, it is no less flung on to our mental sky with a mysterious power to rule us and to prevent us working out our own salvation with diligence.

When our last projection is withdrawn and digested what do we see remaining in the spiritual firmament ? A multitude of gods and godlings, of all ages, forms and standing in the divine hierarchy. Brahma, Shiva, and Vishnu, each with a hundred variations; God the Father, Son and Holy Ghost; Ahura-Mazda, Jehovah, Allah and the vast assortment of gods of the orient. all are now seen as the products of the human mind, as signs and at the same time healing symbols of his undevelopment. From the savage's sacred tree with which he is still in a *participation mystique*, as Lévy-Bruhl called it, through the gods of Olympus to the trival and national Gods of the Theist religions, all, says the Buddhist, exist, but all alike are 'bound upon the Wheel' and have not yet attained deliverance. And devils are as many as the gods, for the Devil is only God reversed, the shadow of the light. The worship of the one and the propitiation of the other is alike a sign of weakness, and all these entities can screen the eyes of man from the Truth which he claims to seek. The same applies to religions, which are man-made forms of apparatus for the worship of some God. These may be rafts, to be used to cross the stream of life and to be left behind on reaching the other shore, or they may be shields from the truth which the seeking mind is unable to face when found. In the same way the god may be a substitute for the effort needed to stand alone. To use a crutch knowing it to be a crutch is one thing; to use it while claiming to walk unaided is a lie to oneself, which is the worst form of lie.

Perhaps the attitude of every man in regard to God is one of the two following: to project the highest concept one can form of the Absolute, and to expand it as understanding is advanced with use, or to effect a double process, on the one hand leaving the Absolute as such, unknown and unknowable, and on the other hand finding it and using it as a force, a cosmic and unlimited force, within.

The latter method, surely preferable, is that of the Buddhist, whereas the former is more usual with the Bhakti yogin. For the Absolute is absolute and there can be no bridge between it and the relative. Being absolute it cannot be expressed or described, and all words concerning it are futile. As Eckhart said, 'Whatever thou sayest of God is untrue', and in older Chinese words, 'the Tao that can be expressed is not the eternal Tao'. If it be argued that the Absolute itself is a concept, to our relative minds it is necessary. In Buddhist terms, 'There is an Unborn, Unbecome, Unmade, for were it not for this there would be no escape from birth, becoming, making.' At least this thought of the Absolute is the highest thinking possible on God. The greatest minds of the earth have from the earliest days attempted to express their vision of this Absolute, and in anthologies like Aldous Huxley's *Perennial Philosophy* their views, enormously diverse in form but one in substance, are collated for the thinking world to see. But about this One which is beyond the one and the many the Buddha observed a 'thundering silence'.

Only when the mind falls back, exhausted, utterly frustrated in attempts to know what may not by the processes of thought be known, does it look for substitutes, for symbols to express the inexpressible. Realizing that thought can never take the pilgrim to the goal of ultimate awareness, the Buddhist pilgrim points to the Way which the All-Awakened One proclaimed 2,500 years ago. This leaves unprofitable thoughts aside, and strives to develop in mind the faculty, which alone can know the Absolute, the intuition, the 'third eye' of direct awareness by which the part and the whole are known as one, and the Absolute is seen in each of its infinite and ever-changing forms.

For one who treads this Path no lesser God than the Absolute is needed. The Buddha and those of lesser mind who teach the same transcendent journey, are for him guides, not gods, human beings who in the many have found THAT. But man is lazy, frightened and psychologically immature. He cries out for a crutch in his walking, for a Saviour to bear, or share with him in bearing, the burdens which are none the less heavy for being self-imposed. He prefers to project his insufficiencies and to worship, plead with, bribe a self-created God to bear the effects of his causes. Hence Theist religions of every kind, from the tribal God of a 'savage' to the infinite complexity of the Hindu pantheon which is yet, in the mind of the cultured Indian, a pattern of manifestation of the one primordial Brahman. Even in Buddhism there has been a fall from the supreme position, and in corners of the Buddhist field may be found the 'services' with prayers and pleading which the Buddha would have condemned as forming no part of the Way.

Yet there is truth in Theism, and the Buddhist who has learnt to work out his own salvation can see its uses for others not so strong. Having himself achieved a vision of the God Transcendent he is aware of the Immanence by which the Absolute abides in every blade of grass, and is throned eternally within his own most human mind. With all the universe within him, and all its strength, compassion, wisdom and beauty at his command, he looks to no god between himself and his own Absolute, but can look with understanding on the man that needs a crutch upon the Way, and will even carve it for him. The less developed soul—in the Buddhist sense, that compound of conflicting attributes which moves from life to life towards Enlightenment—has need of a rope with which to pull itself up the mountain, of a god who, placed ahead on the Path, will call to him and draw him on. So God is invented, endowed with attributes which, splendid or painfully human, are yet the reflection of the creating mind, and given the power (which could not be given were it not in the mind which gave it) to save the climber from his sins, and to lead him to that Enlightenment which, did he know it, dwells untarnished, only waiting to be found within.

But this God should be flexible in form, and should be allowed to grow. To the baby the mother is God; then the father. Then projection is flung further, on to a teacher or leader: then the godhead is dissolved into an abstraction and 'God', very vague and rather frightening, is born. As the camera may be fixed at three feet, six feet, twenty-four feet and so on into infinity, and the eyes are focused from the point of the nose out to the sky, so the Power within is projected outward, and for the greater part of our unthinking lives we are content with *tariki* as the Japanese call it, looking for salvation to some Other Power, until with growing awareness we turn to *jiriki*, salvation by Self-power, and find from self-experience that Nirvana and Samsara are one.

The ideal, to change the analogy, should always move ahead of us, and God be a condensation of thought and feeling of the best of our ambitions not yet realized. For God, once seen as concept, is subject to change, as all else in the universe; only an unchanging God is a stumbling block, for nothing *is* save the Absolute, and not until the pilgrim, his God and the Absolute are one may the trinity dissolve in actual awareness. The rest is silence.

The Buddhist, then, ignores the Absolute as beyond conception, and walks on toward an actual awareness of THAT which is beyond thought. He is content to wait until he reaches the mountain top before demanding knowledge of its nature or of the view which is then revealed. Meanwhile he looks into the deeps of his own mind for all that he needs upon this Way and finds it. As is said in *The Voice of Silence*, 'Look within; thou art Buddha', and as the Zen Patriarch Hui-Neng pointed out, 'So far as the Buddha nature is concerned, there is no difference between an enlightened man and an ignorant one. What makes the difference is that one realizes it and the other does not.'

The alternative attitude to the Absolute has, to the Buddhist, no appeal—to project to some point between the human mind and Reality, the part and the Whole, a concept which is built of man-made attributes, and then to worship it. In the Buddhist pantheon such a god is less than man, deserving at his hands no more respect than the other ranks of gods and godlings, such as nature-forces, personified aspects of the cosmic law and the like. Certainly none is worthy of worship for none possesses an influence on the lives of men which man has not in the first place given it.

The steady withdrawal of these and other projections is therefore essential to the Western Buddhist before he can make any progress on the Way. As the process continues he will be amused and perhaps annoyed to discover how many and various are those not yet withdrawn. Moreover, he will, in time, discover that the God which he thought had been utterly destroyed is not only a product of the conscious mind but also of the dark unconscious, not merely a creation of thought but a projection of mental material which is still below its horizon. What then? Our mental evolution would seem to necessitate the slow consumption by the tiny conscious mind of the as yet vast unconscious. Yet we must consciously consume that 'thing' within the mind that we knew as God without developing the *folie de grandeur* or imagining that hereby we become that God. For while it is true that each part, as it grows, increasingly becomes the Whole, and the 'soul' does become 'God', this mystical process is one of humility and never of pride. The fool claims to be *a* God. The Buddhist knows that this path is a cul-de-sac and leads to spiritual insanity. Only as the self dies and makes room for Sunyata, the Void which alone is full, does the part re-become the whole.

What happens when this God-idea, part thought-produced and part the child of the unconscious, is at last withdrawn and consumed? First, there is a vast sense of relief, an inrush of light as when one cuts down a large dark tree which grew right up to the window. Then comes balance, as the weight of responsibility swings back over one's own two feet and is no longer leant against an outside object. The tension of emotion is released when there is no more an outside thing which calls for love, fear, adoration, expectation or an uncomfortable compound of all these and other emotions. In its place is a universe which, though clearly an illusion is, in a relative world, the child of law. In his 'walking on' the pilgrim now knows where he is, and where he is going, and although he will have to battle on the way with a vast assortment of powers, of fate and fortune, blind terror and cold doubt, he will know these to be forces of his own unconscious, and learn to cope with them as they come.

If the destruction of the God complex is complete, and no Buddhist substitute of Dharma-kaya or Amida is allowed to fill the gap, the pilgrim will be a little frightened and then delighted to observe that he has left himself no Saviour of any kind. He will not need one. Increasingly aware of the identity of every living thing, and none is dead, in the world of *maya* around him, his Bodhisattva compassion for every form of life will become increasingly genuine and therefore powerful. Bereft of God he will find Sunyata, the Void which underlies phenomena, the restful nothingness which is the essence of each 'thing'. His focus will shorten; he will learn to find everything in each, to see that all means are ends in themselves of equal importance, and that the part, in its essential partness, is indeed the whole.

On the Way he will create, use and let go a number of teachers, points of wider view, half-gods and great ideals; but he will never stop. Yet the Absolute will more and more invade him, not at his will but with its own. Here only is the meaning of the Japanese *tariki*, salvation by Other Power, but when that power is found it is found within and it is one with the All-Power which is, though manifest before our eyes, unconquerably Absolute.

Beyond diversity lies unity, first as a concept and then as experience. Beyond unity lies THAT which is beyond unity and diversity. Beyond THAT is silence. It is somewhere in this superb experience that the moment of Truth will come. When this consumes us utterly and no whimper of self is left we shall know God as he is, Unborn, Uncompounded, beyond any name. Thereafter we must learn to live accordingly.

Said a Sufi sage to another, 'I have never seen anything without seeing God therein'. Said the other, 'I have never seen anything but God'.

14

Phase Two: 'Stop Thinking'

Phase One was largely destructive, loosening adhesions to past thought. We now pass to the control of thought. On the basic assumptions that we must develop and use thought to the limit in order to transcend its limitations, that there is no by-pass round the intellect nor any short-cut to Enlightenment, we must learn to choose what we think, to stop 'being thought' by outside pressure, to disentangle consciousness from the machines it uses and their products.

To this end we must learn to harness and ride the stallions of thought and to cease being dragged round the ring of Samsara by them. This is intensely difficult, so difficult that most so-called systems of meditation are really no more than methods to this end. True meditation, as we shall see later, is the deliberate use of a controlled mind to spiritual ends. The operative word is control.

For the moment we must turn to metaphysics, the spiritual truths of which physics in its largest form is the material counterpart. As the Master Huang Po says in the opening statement of his recorded sermons, 'All the Buddhas and all sentient beings are nothing but the One-Mind, beside which nothing exists. . . . This One-Mind alone is the Buddha, and there is no distinction between the Buddha and sentient beings but that sentient beings are attached to forms and so seek externally for Buddhahood.' Whether Western scholars call this mysticism or the philosophy of Absolute Idealism is of no importance. To all who have achieved Zen experience it is completely true.

Much follows, but for us three observations may be enough. First, that to achieve Mind-Only we need to develop Prajna-intuition, and this is a long process involving the transcending of thought. Let us repeat, that the process is gradual; only when the 'hundred-foot pole', or the pair of steps, is climbed to the top will come the sudden leap into Zen awareness. Secondly, we shall derive much help from the philosophic background of Zen teaching, the vast field of literature collectively known as the Prajna-paramita, 'the Wisdom that has gone Beyond'. Very great minds wrote it; only great minds fully understand it. If the greatest Western exponent of it, Dr Edward Conze, has done what he can to make some of it available in translation, and others, such as Professor T. R. V. Murti, have done what they can to make it under-standable, it remains what it seems to be, the highest level of thought yet achieved by man.

Complementary to this Madhyamika School of Nagarjuna is the Mind-Only School which expresses its teaching in terms of what the West calls psychology. The two schools agree that there is nothing but the One-Mind, and that it is void of all predicates, all attributes, all things. It is. But just as 'the Unborn, Unoriginated, Unformed' breathed out, as the Hindus say, and 'thought' the manifested universe we call Samsara, so we, with our individual minds think each our lesser thoughts of high or low degree and are responsible for them.

And thirdly, our minds are remarkably dual in function, the higher and lower aspects being as distinct in practice as the difference between, say, the physical plane and our feelings. We must learn to control the lower mind, develop the higher mind which moves in the field of abstract truths, and so awaken the intuition by which alone we shall *know* the truths of Zen. For those who like analogies, we must climb from the fog-laden base of the valley floor up to increasing sunlight, a wider view, a purer air until at the summit, with a total view in all directions we see the sun of Buddha-mind flooding the earth and sky.

Let us to work. We are not suppressing thought but learning to think only as we will. This involves dissociation from clamorous thoughts, detachment from them, the power to refuse admission to them when they come. As someone wittily put it, 'I cannot prevent the birds from flying over my head, but I *can* prevent their making nests in my hair'.

Enlightened persons will no doubt remark once more that all this is waste of time. Why cleanse the mind when it is already pure? I for one patiently repeat that it is not pure. Mind-Only is pure; our minds are not yet Buddha-mind, only potentially so. Let us to work.

To control thought we must see what it is.

Every thought is a separate product of what we vaguely refer to as the mind. It is the child of imagining, meaning image-making, and all visible things are first made in the mind as images and then clothed in matter. A holiday, a business deal, an invitation to lunch are all alike born in the imagination. In an ideally controlled thought-machine they are pure of interference by personal, selfish desire (*kama*), which

127

strives to drag down thought to the level of its own illusion, while the power of Prajna-intuition exerts its influence to raise the level of consciousness to its own world of enlightenment, the impersonal realm of Buddha-mind, Mind-Only.

In our present sadly uncontrolled machine it is truer to agree with the Master K. H. as quoted by A. P. Sinnett in *The Occult World*, 'Man is continually peopling his current in space with a world of his own, crowded with the offspring of his fancies, desires, impulses and passions, a current which reacts upon any sensitive or nervous organization which comes in contact with it, in proportion to its dynamic intensity.' The duration and power of the thought will depend on the clarity of its conception, the strength of will informing it and its repetition in the course of thought-habit. Its effect will follow the motive behind the creating will. Each such thought is a 'thing', having its own substance which, though invisible to the physical eye, may be seen by those with a slightly higher range of vision, and the Tibetans at least have developed the power of seeing what they build in thought for use in their own religious practices. It can be used, as all other power, for good or evil. The good is present in good-will, in healing thoughts and blessing; the evil, wrought by hate, by certain forms of thought-transference, by the abuse of mob-oratory, and by the utterly evil practices of 'brain-washing'. This is the greatest power in the possession of man. It has been said that there is no force on earth more powerful than that of a thought whose time has come. (What else was the abolition of slavery, or the United Nations or Marxism?) The exercise of thought can be deliberate, as used in high or low degree in daily affairs, or merely the uncontrolled reaction of the mind to outside or indeed to inside stimulus. And when the thought moves on in the normal cycle of birth, growth, decay and death it will die and, as set out in Phase One, be either pushed into the unconscious or remain as distorting factor in our handling of new thoughts as they arise.

Let us apply this to our present phase. Remember the link between each thought, whether or not charged with feeling, and the father-mind. All thoughts make Karma, that is, produce an effect which will react on the thinker and then on all mankind. All conditioning is Karma visible. We *are*, it must be many times repeated, what we have made ourselves in thought, and our task is to extract ourselves from its embrace.

Let us look more closely at a thought. Its nature is to divide, by comparison, distinction and then by added approval or disapproval. A thought can never be utterly true for it is achieved by limitation—

a choice of this or that of a million attributes. To define is to limit; a definition stops and kills the life-force of the thought. A description can never in itself transmit experience, nor can any body of thoughts, even the conglomerate mass of thought called 'Buddhism'. Thoughts, like feelings, handle only the products of direct experience, which strangely enough comes only to us through the senses and the intuition, the bottom and top, one may say, of our contact with the world about us and within. Truly 'the Mind is the slayer of the Real', as *The Voice of the Silence* puts it. So 'let the disciple slay the slayer'! Huang Po as usual puts the case most pithily. 'The ignorant eschew phenomena but not thought, the wise eschew thought but not phenomena.' Zen *is*. Zen is concerned only with direct experience, either of the intuition, by way of the experience of Satori, or by the other end of the spectrum, as it were, on the physical plane. 'When hungry I eat; when tired I sleep.'

It follows surely that while at best the intellect is a magnificent machine for reaching and expressing truth about the world of relativity it can never directly *know*, and so merge the enquirer, his enquiry and the object sought in one entire experience. This is the prerogative of the intuition, its unique function, purpose and power.

We must examine certain uses of thought which in particular we must control. The first is our habit of projection, as Carl Jung first made it known in the West. 'Our ordinary psychological life is swarming with projections. You can find them spread out in the newspapers, rumours and in ordinary social gossip. . . . We are certain we know what other people think. . . . We are convinced that certain people have all the bad qualities we do not know in ourselves.' We blame everything under the sun for our own mistakes and shortcomings. All else are at fault but never we ourselves. The man who will shoulder his own responsibilities, take the blame for his own error, is a man indeed. "He lives in the house of self-collection." Such a man knows that whatever is wrong in the world is in himself, and if he only learns to deal with his own shadow then he has done something real for the world. He has succeeded in removing an infinitesimal part at least of the unsolved social problems of our day.'

We shall not do this by stopping our mental processes. Mere 'sitting' is not acquiring mind-control. Hui-Neng puts it brutally: 'To stop the working of the mind and to sit quietly in meditation is a disease and not Zen.' Even Samadhi is but a stage on the way. 'Sila, Samadhi, Prajna', runs the Zen message. Sila, morality or character-building comes first; Samadhi as a high degree of mind-control should follow, and *then*

Prajna, the break-through out of present mind to the No-mind of Enlightenment.

Thirdly, we shall need the whole of our mind-power to break through to No-mind, and at present we are sadly wasting it. Phiroz Mehta has long attacked our habit of 'mental chattering'. The power wasted is that of a racing engine, a daily leakage of force which is urgently needed by the would-be concentrated mind. If we are to raise, as one of our members says, 'a head of steam' to achieve a break-through we cannot waste the pressure we are trying to build. Hence R. H. Blyth's tremendous statement: 'Think of Zen, of the Void, of Good and Evil, and you are bound hand and foot. Think only and entirely and completely of what you are doing at the moment and you are as free as a bird.'

We must learn at least to slow down our reaction to outside stimulus, as that of advertisements, news in the press or idle chatter. We can refuse to be interested in matters which are not our concern. We can stop arguing which, as Hui-Neng says, 'implies a desire to win, strengthens egotism and ties us to the belief in the idea of a permanent "self"'. We can stop hurting others by spiteful or even thoughtless words.

If this affects our social life, what of it? We are concerned with the Zen life, not with our one-time friends' behaviour and their views on us. As Sohaku Ogata wrote, 'Zen is a way of life based on a new point of view', that of Non-duality, and to achieve it we must sacrifice, and readily, much of the small talk, fruitless chatter, idle criticism in which we spend so much of our present life.

We must learn to be vulnerable to criticism, ignorant where we have no wish to know; to admit we do not understnad what we wish we did, including Buddhism. Can we be more 'mindful and self-possessed' at all times of the day; our minds in neutral unless deliberately put in gear; able as a tortoise to withdraw from objects to subjective life within; to rest more at the centre without hope or fear, desire or hate, and without particular views?

Let us make friends with silence, at 'the still centre of the turning world.' Then will a new power manifest, the light of the intuition shining through. We shall more readily use the instrument of thought as we now use a lawn-mower, a tape-recorder or a car. The self, of course, will intervene with a hundred methods of frustration. Let it die, as 'the three fires' of hatred, lust and illusion. Make friends with self for it is not easily slain. But it can be starved of its food of selfishness, and die because its owner is just too busy to attend to it. Try it!

Meanwhile ask yourselves the Questions formulated in the syllabus.

1. *Can I now for minutes on end stop all reaction to outside events or objects, whether news or views or events? And the same with thoughts that flow into the mind unbidden. Can I cease at will from 'mental chattering'?*

2. *Can I stop approving or disapproving of everything which others do or say, whether I express my feelings or no? Can I really mind my own business?*

3. *Have I the moral strength to refuse to form an opinion about happenings around me or at large? And can I frankly change an opinion once formed?*

4. *Can I let the waves of thought die down and learn to 'be still and know that I am God', i.e. the Buddha-Mind within?*
   And am I now content to be alone at times with silence, and even prefer it, dwelling consciously at 'the still centre of the turning world', and remain in this condition back in the noisy world?

15

Meditation: An Interlude

So far we have considered the large body of thoughts, abandoned or still to some extent in use, to which we are strongly attached. We have realized the range and power of these adhesions and the extent to which they make a mockery of the ideal, 'to let the mind abide nowhere'. Then we considered the thought-machine and the nature of its products, thoughts, concepts, ideas. We looked at a thought, saw that it had size, shape, duration and karmic effect, on ourselves as its creator and, with diminishing effect on all. We watched this instrument, the intellect, producing thoughts in vast variety, some as willed but most, to our shame, in automatic reaction to outside or inside stimulus. All this work on thought was done with thought. It has no spiritual importance, but that which remains to be done could not be done without it.

As soon as the thought-machine is taken in hand, as the most powerful faculty in the average Western mind, we are faced with the age-old practice of meditation. If the aim of all Zen training be, as here suggested, to reach the end of thought and then, by the power of the thought-machine itself, to break out of its limitations into Prajna-awareness, a direct vision of 'things as they are', then any and all means to this tremendous end must be considered. In Zen the place of meditation is presumably central, for the word is a corruption of the Chinese Ch'an, a variation of the Sanskrit Dhyana which, if any English word can suffice, means meditation. Indeed, the Zen School is still described in certain text-books as the Meditation School of Buddhism.

The word meditation covers a wide variety of practice. Here it is used to mean the deliberate use of a controlled mind to a specific spiritual end, the wakening of the faculty of the Prajna-intuition, which is as clearly beyond the intellect as the intellect is beyond or different from feeling or the physical plane.

In one form or another meditation has been used in schools of spiritual training from time immemorial. Every school of mysticism,

132

be it Persian, Indian or Buddhist, knows it, and Christian prayer, stripped of its inessential use of a hypostatic personal God, is meditation in another form.

We are here concerned, however, with Buddhism, and in particular with one school of it, Ch'an or Zen. Study of the Theravada method of Vipassana, elaborated in the Pali Abhidhamma, will be found of value in any attempt at mental training, and at the other extreme of method is the Tibetan form of ritual visualization, equally difficult for the Western mind. In Zen there are two schools, that of Rinzai Zen which is known to the West through the writings of Dr D. T. Suzuki, and that of Soto Zen of which little is known in Europe, and even as known seems to have little appeal. By Zen meditation, therefore, we mean that of the Rinzai School.

This is very different, at least in avowed aim, from other forms. As Mrs Beatrice Lane Suzuki, herself an expert in certain aspects of Japanese Buddhism, wrote in a little-known work, *Impressions of Mahayana Buddhism*, 'Zen meditation differs from general meditation as we understand it in Western treatises, New Thought, Catholic and others, in that it is not a letting of the mind dwell upon a thought . . . and an endeavour to realize its meaning. Neither is it like certain Eastern practices which seek to stop the flow of thought and enjoy nothingness. Zen meditation is for the purpose of identifying oneself with the highest reality. We are so accustomed in the West to think that meditation means to think of the goodness of God, or to take up some high thought and consider it with the wish to incorporate it in our character. On the contrary, Zen would have us put all such thoughts aside.' Mrs Suzuki then goes on to say that some support for the mind is nevertheless necessary, and hence the creation and development of the koan system in China, later adopted in Japan. But if we in the West are not to use the koan system, for reasons already sufficiently described, what shall we use 'to support the mind' while striving to identify our-selves with the 'highest reality'? I boldly reply that such a purpose, often described as 'to seek the Self', or 'to merge in the Buddha-mind' is still to be bound in phrases, without value unless the student can be led by a series of gradual steps to a sudden awareness of what they mean.

For there is no such 'thing' as the highest reality, or the Self or, indeed, the Buddha-Mind. These phrases mean no more than the raising of consciousness to the level on which it sees that it is and always has been Buddha-Mind. As *The Voice of the Silence* puts it, 'Look within, thou art Buddha'. Or in the words of the Master Huang

133

Po, 'All the Buddhas and all sentient beings are nothing but the One Mind, beside which nothing exists'. Or, in Christian terms, 'I and my Father are one'.

This is why all talk of attainment is dangerously misleading. There is nothing to attain and nothing to attain it. There is, however, a long journey on the way to seeing, in pure experience, that this is true. Hence the process, advocated here, of thought-control and mind-development leading to 'illumined thought', and thence to the first 'peeps' of a true vision of things as they are.

Already the student will have found the value of perpetual 'mindfulness', a key-term in the Abhidhamma. But before he can use the mind for meditation he must bring it under control. Before we can drive a car to Brighton, we must learn to drive a car. Hence the practice of concentration must precede the practice of meditation which is, it may be repeated, the application to a prescribed purpose of a controlled mind. The best known exercise to this end is that of 'watching the breath', as it enters and leaves the nose, the purpose of which is to see that meanwhile no *other* thought enters the mind. Such power of concentration is, however achieved, known to every man who has reached success in the life of the community. Without considerable thought-control the human has not moved beyond the consciousness of the animal whence his body came.

Meditation, however, in all its forms is profoundly different. For the first time the controlled mind is being harnessed to spiritual ends. Let us look, then, to the purpose of meditation. Many students would describe their own as 'to calm the mind', and in this they would have the support of the Master Hui-Neng, who said that 'to meditate means to realize inwardly the imperturbability of the Essence of Mind'. And this accords with the high ideal set out in the Bhagavad Gita, to achieve 'an unwavering steadfastness of heart upon the arrival of every event whether favourable or unfavourable'. Others would answer, 'to see the the Way more clearly', and it is difficult to travel upon any Path without some vision of what the journey means and the nature of the end of it. Others, perhaps more introvert in temperament, would speak of the development of character, not mentioned as a proper purpose by Mrs Suzuki. And the rest ? 'To find the Self', or 'the Buddha within'.

This last is on the face of it conceded to be admirable, for if followed in the fullness of its meaning it avoids the major danger of making meditation an end instead of what it should be, a means, one of many, to the awakening of Prajna. Yet even this is not right purpose. We must emphasize again that we are not concerned to attain anything, for there is nothing to attain. We may wish to be free, but if so from what? 'Free from the illusion that we are not free', as R. H. Blyth puts it. The Lama Trungpa was right when he wrote in *Medition in Action*, 'Meditation is dealing with purpose itself. Medition is not for something but is dealing with its aim. . . . The whole idea of meditation is to develop an entirely different way of dealing with things, where you have no purpose at all.' Here is the Zen ideal of purposelessness. As Dr Suzuki put it, translating from Hui-Neng, 'There is within oneself that which knows and thereby one has a satori.'

But if this be the purpose of meditation, ideally conceived, what should be its motive? For the two are very different. Purpose is concerned with what we are trying to do; motive decides why we do it. There is surely only one 'right' motive, the benefit of all mankind. Whether in reaching this one uses the ideal of the Arhat or that of the Bodhisattva, in the end no effort for oneself alone is fruitful, for early on the path the realization comes that there is no self to be enlightened. Once this is understood the problem of the ego and its largely animal desires is solved. There is Buddha-Mind, manifesting in a million forms. There is the needful personality, the four lower *skandhas* of basic Buddhism, but there is also consciousness, clothed in a complex 'Self' or character, a child of the Absolute, the user of the personality, which moves from life to life, ever learning from past error, ever moving upward to reunion with the 'Unborn, Unconditioned' whence it came. None of these is the ego of Western thought. This is illusion, or, as it has been put, 'just a silly idea', the belief that 'I' have interests different from and incompatible with all other 'I's, that I can usefully strive for my own aggrandisement to the detriment of all other forms of the One Life-principle. Once we drop this fond illusion most of our suffering falls away and man—tripartite, so it seems—is free to move as fast as may be towards an awareness, not his but pure awareness, of 'things as they are'. In this raised consciousness all opposites are seen as the twin appearances of an inseverable, universal process, a return to the Source, the Buddha-Mind which alone is.

Meditation, then, has high ambition. It has its corresponding dangers and it is unwise to ignore them. The beginner is apt to strain himself into illness or a sudden revulsion in which he gives it up, but to strain is as foolish here as in physical exercise. More subtle, and often unnoticed by the meditator, is a psychological process by which a brief and trifling experience is claimed as 'Enlightenment'. In this case the force tends to fire back, as it were, into the illusionary ego, and the man concerned will not be budged from what, to others, is an utterly false belief. On the contrary, he may set himself up as a teacher and lead the blind into the folly of his own blindness.

Thirdly, there can be an awakening of psychic powers, which is frankly the aim of some who take up meditation, or at least their secret desire. Here is folly indeed, for it is almost certain that such powers will be abused by using them for personal ends, and the karmic effect of such misuse of power is terrible. And finally, there seems to be a natural law, to some extent explained by Western theories on the unconscious mind, that spiritual effort in advance of mankind precipitates what can be called unripe or unexpended karma. Only this explains the dreadful, unexpected happenings which often meet the would-be pilgrim on the Way. The serious meditator must expect and suffer this unpleasantness, work through it and walk on.

As to a teacher, we in the West will not for a while have Masters for our guidance. We must earn them, whether a guru in the Indian sense, or a monk for those who hold that only a man in a special robe is qualified for the task, or a mere layman who may in fact be thoroughly competent. But all have limitations, and many are apt to teach their own particular method and to insist that it is the sole right way. There is no 'right way' to meditate, though there may be many which are undesirable. The meditator must find his own way, and as soon as possible realize that the only true Teacher is within. If I may summarize a passage from Sokei-an Sasaki Roshi, 'In meditation you separate yourself from your environment and realize the Buddha in yourself. The Master is in *here*. You have but to knock at the door and ask to meet the Master. The answer comes from the inside. But to call you must make an effort, must knock at the door of your heart. And remember the door of the temple is not the Master. Many people think that concentration and meditation are Buddhism.' Here, then, is the final danger, already mentioned. Meditation is at best a means and not in itself an end. To some extent all meditation is unnatural, and no 'sitting' for however long will itself produce enlightenment. Zen masters of old never tired of pointing out the futility of mere sitting in the sense of Dhyana, and Hui-Neng emphasizes throughout his famous sutra that Dhyana is but a means for the wakening of Prajna, direct awareness of Reality. From Matsu's story of the futility of polishing a tile to turn it into a mirror, to the works of the late Dr Suzuki, the Masters have attacked mere sitting 'as being fixed compared with the constant mobility of life itself, because it does not belong to the native activity of the mind'. Certainly it is a forced growth, and all such is dangerous. Nevertheless the practice has its value for those Western Buddhists who, not content with study alone, want a careful blend of study, meditation and application with which to prepare the mind for direct experience.

On the numerous methods of meditation there is no need to elaborate here. If not for long hours, as in the koan exercise of Japan, there remains the popular method of a regular period of time each day, preferably in the same place. As to the theme or subject, let us wait for Phase Three of our syllabus. For the few, there is the ideal of meditation all the day, the cultivation of a state of mind in which consciousness is deliberately raised whenever it is not chained to lower purposes, and used as a searchlight in the darkness of Ignorance. This is the highest form of mindfulness, what the Lama Trungpa called 'working meditation, where wisdom and skilful means must be combined as the two wings of a bird.' Only a mind so poised can be said to 'abide nowhere'.

This practice, of all day mindfulness, even if modestly acquired, is better even than the daily period fixed in time and place. As Trevor Leggett wrote in *A First Zen Reader*, 'Withdrawing into meditation, and then advancing and handling affairs, this advancing and withdrawing, movement and rest, together, must be Zen.' In such a way one may be busily and happily 'walking on', 'living life as life lives itself', as Dr Suzuki calls it, flowing with one's karma and laughing all the time.

Meditation

Withdraw the mind. Be still. Be no more there.
Far on the rim of some unfelt
Unheard horizon earth revolves
In toil and tumult of affray.
Be still and be not anywhere.

Withdraw. Far off, mankind in love's despite
With warm entanglement would snare
The feet of sense. Be unaware.
With folded hands be silent now
And see with closed eyes the Darkness-Light.

Now distance only, and a void of things
And yet the infinite in either hand.
In poise, without desire or no desire
Be absolute for life, a mind set free
Abiding nowhere, on two wings.

16

Phase Three: Re-think

Having lossened our attachment to existing thoughts, and begun to control the machine of thought itself, we boldly feed into the mind a new series of living ideas. These, it is claimed because it has been proved by some, will steadily raise consciousness, via 'illumined thought' to the end of thought's limitations, to the abolition of the screen that thought creates between the mind and direct experience of reality.

Let us ask again, is such a process in the face of the Zen masters? The answer is apparently yes but actually no. It is said of Zen that it abhors abstractions. It certainly does so in the sense of vague generalizations having no immediate relation with our concrete world. Intellectualism, in the sense of an erection of ideas between the seer and what he strives to see, is of course the death of the Zen experience. But careful reading of the masters' literature shows the distinction in their minds between dead doctrine and living ideas, and Dr Suzuki himself, who gave the West its knowledge of Zen in a score of books which speak, as all words must, on the plane of the intellect, agrees that philosophy is a necessary background and companion for training for Zen experience. He was attacked in Japan for reducing Zen to the level of the intellect, and writing of that which cannot be described. His answer was clear, that to rouse Prajna (Wisdom), the intuition and the intellect go hand in hand. In a hitherto unpublished manuscript he writes, 'Inasmuch as we are living in the world of the sense-intellect, and so constituted as to ask questions at every situation we meet, there is nothing wrong in our resorting to our intelligence and trying to find a solution intellectually. What Zen objects to is taking the intellect as the sole agency for some sort of solution to every question we raise. It is of the nature of the intellect to probe into the mysteries of life, but it is a grave mistake to trust it absolutely, or to think that it gives satisfaction, especially when the questions are concerned with our being itself.' Such questions he explains, do not come out of the intellect in its own right but from a much deeper source than curiosity. 'When intellectualized, Being is no more itself. Hence its unattainability. The deepest spiritual satisfaction that follows it must come from this fact of unattainability, which must be preserved undisturbed by our intellectual agitation. The Unattainable must be left to itself until it is ready to give an answer, which comes apparently from the intellect but which is in fact the outcome of the intellect being instigated by the Unattainable. The more the commotions the deeper the satisfaction. This is the mystery of being and we rest contented in its "isness".' Finally, in this profound passage, Dr Suzuki begs the reader not to put intellection on one side and the Unattainable on the other. 'Do not let them stand in opposition. When the Unattainable is taken in as unattainable, it ceases to be an unattainability. Whatever opposition there was in the beginning between the attainable and Unattainable, between the knowable and the Unknowable, between conceptualization and Reality is no more obtainable. This is called the Zen experience.' He ends by pointing out that this experience 'does not itself take place on the conceptual plane but existentially or experientially, not statically but dynamically'.

Surely this is the answer to those who complain of an approach to Zen via the intellect? The intellect may, and in the West surely must be used, but the user must know the limitations of his chosen tool. The intellect is a magnificent instrument but it has been brightly said that its highest thought will ever be that Truth is beyond all thinking!

Study, then, is right, with some meditation to help digest the wisdom so obtained, and daily application will bring to earth the abstractions of our study. We must work as research students as distinct from memory examinees, seeking original proof of the truth of every teaching by all available means. It seems to follow that the better developed the machine of study the higher the principles which can be studied, and the sooner the Beyond of the intellect may be attained.

We need not be afraid of the grandeur of the truth we study. As Dogen, the founder of Soto Zen in Japan, wrote of meditation, 'Think the Unthinkable. How do you think the Unthinkable? Think beyond thinking and unthinking. That is the important aspect of sitting.' We are tempted to add, 'Not just sitting!' The importance of original research cannot be overstressed. 'Truth repeated,' says Aldous Huxley in *Adonis and the Alphabet*, 'is no longer truth; it becomes truth again only when it has been realized by the speaker as an immediate experience.' He defines well the distinction between knowledge and intuitive understanding. 'Knowledge is acquired when we succeed in fitting a new experience into the system of concepts based upon our old experience. Understanding comes when we liberate ourselves from the old and so make possible a direct unmediated contact with the new, the mystery, moment by moment, of our existence.'

Now, the mind, as we have seen, and all know from experience, functions at two levels or, in modern terms, on two wave-lengths. The lower mind of daily use is heavily suffused with *kama*, self-ish desire, and in this muddle of thought/emotion we spend the greater part of our day. The higher, abstract mind is reaching all the while for the next higher faculty, the plane of intuition. The tension between the two parts of the mind is unceasing, the God within and the animal in which it dwells striving for mastery. Here is the battleground of good and evil, conscience, remorse, of ideals at times perceived then lost in the mists of ignorance and low desire. We may rightly scorn the empty clichés of our public and private life, 'peace on earth', 'the brotherhood of man', and the like, yet these very phrases express truths which *on their own plane*, that of Prajna-intuition, are cosmic forces descended from the Unborn, 'living intelligent laws which burst the self', as I have called them.

These great thought-forces are slowly solidifying expressions or manifestations of the one Life-force of the universe, and, as expressed in words, so many descriptions in that lowly medium of the writer's own experience. Let us call them so many flames of the Light of Enlightenment illumining the higher levels of the thinking mind. They are clearly comparable with the 'Ideas' of Greek philosophy and the 'Archetypes' of Jung.

They can never be fully expressed in words, nor toyed with in the laboratory of the philosophic mind. On their own plane their power is enormous. Truly 'ideas rule the world'. As the Master K. H. wrote to A. P. Sinnett, 'As men's minds receive new ideas, laying aside the old and effete, the world will advance; mighty revolutions will spring from them; institutions, creeds and powers will crumble before their onward march. It will be just as impossible to resist their influence when the time comes as to stay the progress of the tide.' And the Master goes on to emphasize what appears here in Phase One, that first 'we must sweep away as much as possible the dross left us by our pious forefathers. New ideas have to be planted on clean places. . . .' Should we not then be pioneers in the digestion of these new ideas and, having ratified them in experience, offer them humbly and clearly to all mankind? They are not new; no truth is new, but the expression of them is ever new, and in that sense every thought is a new creation, to affect mankind for good or ill.

There is no by-pass round the field of thought. We must study, with clear distinctions between playing with an interesting new idea and digesting a cosmic principle. We shall find that our higher understanding will push out thoughts of lower worth, and the level of habitual thought be raised thereby.

The process needs a measure of courage, and one thinks of Carl Jung in his study deciding to face the unconscious in the belief that the attempt might drive him mad. Certainly the ego will fight back for the preservation of its spurious separate existence. But there are safeguards, three at least. In Mahayana Buddhism one reads of the trinity of Sila, Samadhi, Prajna, in that order. First Sila, morality in its widest meaning, for, as Dr Suzuki says, 'the study of Zen requires a great intellectual integrity and strength of character'. Samadhi, a deep quietude of mind which is a legitimate object of meditation, comes next but is not the goal. This is Prajna, the 'third eye' of Zen awareness. Secondly, we are using a ladder to climb, and climbing slowly. Facing the countless pairs of opposites we seek what I called in *Concentration and Meditation* 'the higher third' above and beyond both. I find support in R. H. Blyth's *Zen in English Literature*, 'The word "good" is a relative word opposed to "bad". The word "Good" is absolute and has no contrary.' Again, ' "Love" is what makes the world go round; love is quite another thing.' We shall not injure the mind by such approach but climb with certainty. And thirdly, by accepting the force in a capsule of thought we make it that much easier to digest. Yet every aspect of the Life-force has the power of the Void, the Absolute, behind it, and to accept and live with any aspect of this force is, as someone said, like opening your mouth to take in the Niagara Falls. The results cannot be unnoticed!

Let us look at some of these Thought-forces, remembering that they are not dogmas, they are not specifically Buddhist, and that they must be accepted as near as possible to their own plane, that of Prajna-intuition, Wisdom incarnate.

They are not dogmas, and should never be allowed to settle down in the mind as new forms of authority. Yet they are greater than mere hypotheses and can never be food for argument. They are living intelligent forces emanating from Buddha-Mind and entering yours and mine. They are not purely Buddhist, and will be found described in one form or another in most of the great religions of the world. But even as steam condenses into water and water into ice, so each is powerful according to the level at which it is allowed to occupy the mind, as spirit, concept or mere matter in the sense of outworn phrases in the printed word.

Let us look at a list of seven; the student will soon add many more. These are not koans in the sense of phrases without meaning as used in Japan. Each has meat on it for thought, yet challenges and wakens the intuition. Each is capable of hourly application, of becoming an operative force at every moment of the day.

In the Zen Class four were taken at random and at once resolved themselves into two pairs. (1) Life is One and indivisible, however many its forms. (2) Prajna (Wisdom) and Karuna (Compassion) are one and indivisible, without meaning apart. A second pair, as it seemed to us, is (3) The Universe as total harmony, and he who breaks that harmony being responsible, under the law of Karma, to restore it. Some wove into this the 'Law of laws', compassion. And this worked out in the magnificent, disturbing statement, (4) 'It's all right.' Yes, it is *all Right*!

Three others have an obvious affinity, and may be several statements of the same truth. (5) 'There is no abiding principle in any thing (Anatta)'. (6) 'There is no thing' (Hui-Neng: 'from the first not a thing is'). (7) 'There is Void only but the Void is full.' Someone added, 'It's all down here', which prompted a poem of mine, 'Look down to Heaven'. Here, in this room is the Absolute and all its works, or nowhere. And another, perhaps a corollary of Life is One. (8) 'There is no death.'

But the list is endless, and there is only space in this brief exposition of the course to expand just one of them at length, 'Life is One' and, more briefly, Wisdom/Compassion. 'If Life is One' appeared as Chapter 7 in Part Two. Here is a shorter development of the tremendous theme of Wisdom/Compassion.

17

Wisdom/Compassion

Prajna, Wisdom, is a key term in Buddhism, and according to Dr Suzuki is the ultimate reality itself. 'Prajna-intuition is the totality of things becoming conscious of itself as such.' This intuition only functions 'when finite objects of sense and intellect are identified with the infinite itself'. The author goes on to explain what this means. 'Instead of saying that the infinite sees itself in itself, it is closer to our human experience to say that an object regarded as finite, as belonging in the world of object and subject, is perceived by Prajna from the point of view of infinity. The intellect informs us that the object is finite, but Prajna contradicts, declaring it to be the infinite beyond the realm of relativity. Ontologically this means that all finite objects or beings are possible because of the infinite underlying them.' And he quotes St Paul's mundane vision 'as in a mirror' and Prajna's vision 'face to face'.

'Prajna is therefore far beyond the range of the intellect. It is knowledge of the highest order permitted to the human mind.' Collating a dozen extracts from his writings we learn something of its birth. 'Prajna flashes from the Unconscious yet never leaves it; it remains unconscious of it. This is the sense of saying that "Seeing is no-seeing, and no-seeing is seeing." ' That is why Hui-Neng remarks that 'one who understands this truth is "without thought, without attachment" '.

Thus Prajna seems to be the godhead when it has become God, the One-Mind as first-born of the Unborn, the awareness which is before the One becomes two, and therefore still the Non-duality itself. In terms of our using it, it is 'the highest spiritual power in our possession, that whereby we "see" beyond the range of thought or any dual-rooted function of the human mind'. It is far more than Samadhi, which is passive, far more than Dhyana as made clear in a score of passages by Hui-Neng. It is activity itself but without object. As such it is for us a matter of experience and clearly beyond the ambit of adequate description to the thinking mind.

It is of course its own authority. As immediate direct awareness it sees all things as infinite and the infinite in finite things. Hence Dr Suzuki's great saying, 'There is nothing infinite apart from finite things.' In application it is 'the infinite way of doing finite things', and when so used it is, as pointed out in the *Tao Te Ching*, 'inexhaustible'.

Its other half, its undivided opposite, is Karuna, Compassion. Each is the other viewed through the other's eyes. Hence Dr Suzuki's oft-quoted opening phrase in his second Lecture to the Emperor of Japan. 'There are two pillars supporting the great edifice of Buddhism, Great Wisdom and Great Compassion. The Wisdom flows from the Compassion and the Compassion from the Wisdom, for the two are one.'

But Karuna is itself a force to be wakened, though it can be to some extent induced, I suggest, by constant application of the truth that life is one. It grows, it will be found, with the death of 'I' and with that diminution leave us the more able to understand and to love all beings. R. H. Blyth noted that 'the closer we are to Mind the closer we are to persons', for the unity, in essence, of all is the more clearly perceived.

Perhaps Prajna is more of the head, of the Indian's Jnana Yoga, and Karuna more of the heart, Bhakti Yoga. The head learns; the heart knows what to do. Both meet in the practice of *upaya kausalya*, skilful means of helping all men in a million ways.

But the two are not two virtues closely linked, they are one spiritual force with a dual expression in the world of duality. Whether viewed as positive/negative, passive/active or static/dynamic matters not. Each is incomplete without the other. We do not actually know until we have expressed our knowledge in the service of all; we cannot help mankind with our compassion unless we have the knowledge needed for right action. 'The Zen experience by itself is not enough. It must be rationalized, as it were. It must speak out. It wants to be conscious of itself. To do this Zen has its own way.'

As an undivided pair, born of a common source, we can perhaps distinguish them by relative function, the Wisdom being Enlightenment turned inwards and Compassion the same turned out. Or, as Dr Masunaga puts it, 'the Buddha enlightened himself by great Wisdom and saved all beings by great Compassion.' Dr Suzuki, than whom, after all, we have no greater authority, described the relation more subtly still. In his *Studies in the Lankavatara Sutra* he says that 'Prajna . . . teaches to clear up our intellectual insight from erroneous discriminations and unjustifiable assertions; for when this is done the heart knows by itself how to work out its native virtues.' He developed this many years later in *Zen and Japanese Culture*. 'When Prajna is attained, we have an insight into the fundamental significance of life and of the world, and cease to worry about individual interests and sufferings. Karuna is free to work its way, which means that love, unobstructed by its selfish encumbrances, is able to spread itself over all things.'

Here, then, is a picture of the need to develop Prajna in its aspect of Wisdom, after which Compassion, no longer obstructed by *avidya*, ignorance, or the 'three fires' of hatred, lust and illusion, can set to work to save all beings by its all-embracing power.

Compassion must be sharply distinguished from the human feeling of love. It is Love as a higher third to hate/love, as Truth is beyond truth/falsehood. It is completely impersonal, a fact not easy for many to digest. The Lama Trungpa called it 'selfless warmth'. It is that fascinating thing, a living law, and *The Voice of the Silence* calls it indeed 'the Law of Laws, eternal Harmony, a shoreless universal essence, the light of everlasting right, the law of Love eternal'. It knows no sense of separateness. It is without attachment, thought of sacrifice or duty or reward. Jesus put it highest of all for our digestion. 'A new commandment I give unto you, that ye love one another; as I have loved you, that ye also love one another. By this shall all men know that ye are my disciples, if ye have love one to another.' Would this be so difficult if we lived as if Life *were* one?

The human embodiment of compassion is the Bodhisattva, the creation of the Mahayana school to offset the comparative limitation of the Arhat of the Theravada School. As Dr Suzuki puts it, 'we can never save ourselves unless we save ourselves altogether, as a unit; not just an individual unit but the totality of individual units as a whole—then there comes real compassion'. Hence the Bodhisattva's vow that he will never enter Nirvana 'until the last blade of grass has entered enlightenment.'

But if the object of help, so to speak, is nothing less than all forms of life without exception, we must help with our compassion whatever object comes to hand. Dr Suzuki, in the only passage I know to this effect, says in his *Studies in the Lankavatara Sutra* that the object of gaining an insight into the inner truth of things is really to qualify oneself for social work. In this connection I note what seems to be the Bodhisattva ideal at work in England, in the field in which the Buddhist Society is trying to make Buddhism known. Is not this force behind the recent multiple effort to help the people at large, not merely by

Government measures but with a more awakened social spirit of goodwill? Its expression may be clumsy but is not the spirit there?

Wisdom/Compassion then, the twofold force which flows from the Unborn should, given access to the heart and mind, serve to break down still more adhesions to the self. It has no limit in its application. Joshu, one of the most famous of Zen masters, was asked, 'The Buddha is the enlightened one and teacher of us all. Is he entirely free of all the passions?' 'No,' said Joshu, 'his greatest passion is to save all beings!' And asked where he would go at death he said 'To hell'. Asked why, he said because only there could he be of further service to mankind!

Love, then, in the sense of Compassion with the eyes of Wisdom, is indeed the greatest force we know, and totally and utterly applied all day would change the individual beyond recognition and in time mankind. If it be thought that love is not the stuff for strong practitioners of Zen remember this, the last quotation here of the greatest Bodhisattva of modern times, Dr D. T. Suzuki. The late Father Thomas Merton went to see him in New York and had a long talk with him. 'The last words I remember Dr Suzuki saying (before the usual good-byes) were "the most important thing is Love".'

18

The Bridge

We have approached the boundaries of thought, and see the meaning of Illumined Thought. Now we seek a bridge from the highest thinking to the Beyond of thought. For this we need to develop the Intuition. Our 'gradual' preparation will bear fruit in 'sudden' moments of No-thought or enlightenment. We shall experience the process of conversion, a dedication of our life henceforth to 'spiritual' purposes. As we continue to raise the habitual level of consciousness to live in 'the higher Self', we shall look with new eyes at Zen truths. We shall the better understand paradox, the meaning of Non-duality, and develop an enormous and indestructible sense of fun.

So far we have cleared out the box-room of old thought, learnt in some degree to control the use of new thought, and introduced into this cleansed machine a series of 'Thought-forces' which, as they begin to operate within the mind, produce a field of Illumined Thought. But we have had to distinguish Vijnana, the relative knowledge to be obtained by thought which Dr Suzuki called 'knowledge undifferentiated' and Prajna, the transcendental thought. The former divides Reality into two, subjects and objects, and in this bifurcation there is always an element of contradiction. In brief, 'intellect cannot answer the questions it raises'. We have reached a point at which some utterly new faculty is needed, not merely to see truth in a different form but Truth at its own level.

This is Buddhi, the intuition, which Carl Jung puts at one corner of his fourfold diagram of human faculties, as opposite the senses, the two opposing the pair of intellect and feeling. 'When I look at a picture', says Dr Suzuki, 'the senses perceive it without the medium of a concept. Mediumless perception is called intuition.' Here is subtlety indeed, a fusion of Jung's pair of opposites! By climbing to the apex of the 'higher third' of every pair, by standing at the point from which the pendulum swings to and fro, we at least visualize the promised land of the Beyond of duality. Standing on 'this shore' we gaze at the 'other shore', viewed now as a Beyond of 'this shore' but soon to be known as both and neither, as also the river running between.

Meanwhile we need a bridge, from the relative to the Absolute, from duality to Non-duality, from thought to No-thought. But can there be such a bridge? The plane of Satori can never be reached by rationalistic thought, however ingeniously handled. There is a gap between the two planes, to cross which an existential leap is needed. The Satori plane when once attained is interfused with the intellectual, and can be used to achieve the forms of truth which thought unaided can never attain. The intellect alone can never know more than 'about it and about'. It can never *know*.

The effort made to jump must be enormous. We are called upon to drop the crutches of our learning, to leave the tramlines of the Western route to reality, to give up reason, logic and even what we view as sense; to live happily with unreason, paradox and nonsense. But we are climbing still, and the more quickly when the loaded rucksack of belief is left behind. We can strive to see the 'higher third' of every pair of opposites, that always there is a Good which is absolute and includes without a blush both good and bad, a Beauty which can digest both beauty and ugliness as we conceive them. We must learn to behave 'as if' the Absolute were true. If I *am* the Buddha-Mind incarnate why should I not live as if this fact were true? And we must come to terms with paradox. What else is Christ's remark, 'Give up thy life if thou wouldst live'? And this is basic Buddhism. As Blyth points out, 'The meaning of a paradox escapes the words. Very well, then, instead of further explanations, floundering farther from Reality, let us scorn truth, turn our back on logic, defy consistency, and behold, the intangible is grasped, the unsayable is said.' How to get the goose out of the bottle, without hurting the goose or breaking the bottle? Answer; 'There, it's out!'

However long the approach, the 'moment' must be sudden, and the long dispute between the sudden and gradual schools of Zen Buddhism seems to me utterly ill-founded.

We are moving to the moment of conversion, by a thousand moments leading to the final 'turning about at the seat of consciousness'. Here is the dawn of dedication, a life set upon new values, motive, purposes, a twenty-four hour day for harnessing our powers—and weaknesses—to the end in view, the liberation of all that lives from the bonds of illusion, by means of the light of Enlightenment revealed in each. The prodigal son is turning his face home, the part returns to the Whole.

All this while we are raising the habitual level of consciousness. To the extent that we learn to live in the 'Higher Self', without pausing to define just what this means, much is achieved. The lower self deflates, its voice is lowered. As strength is withdrawn from the desire element in the psyche it is available at the higher levels of the manifold man, and under the direction of the will is harnessed to right action. But here is no new dichotomy, no splitting of the Self. Sri Krishna Prem, in *The Yoga of the Bhagavad Gita*, uses the analogy of the climber, as I do. 'As a climber reaches for a hand-hold on the rock above him and pulls his whole body upwards, so the climber of the Path aspires with all that is best in him, attains a hand-hold on the heights of vision, but then must pull his lower nature upwards till his whole being stands firmly on the summit.' Note that he climbs to the very top 'muddy boots and all.' The Higher Self is the Buddha-Mind. Shall we not enter in, and act accordingly?

For the rest we can but wait. Nothing we do can *cause* a flash of the intuition, still less the mighty break-through of Satori. Here is no cause/effect, for Satori is beyond the plane where cause/effect holds sway. 'The object of Zen discipline is to prepare ourselves for Satori.' We prepare unceasingly, and then while 'walking on', we wait.

While waiting let us climb to the Higher Self and look out through its eyes. Can we now see better that 'all distinctions are falsely imagined', as Hui-Neng put it? All, without exception? 'The table is square,' says R. H. Blyth, 'at the same time it is round. Every thing is relative; at the same time it is absolute'; and it is both *at once*. Blyth in his *Mumonkan* gets very difficult here. 'All affirmation of identity is separation, all denial of difference is separation.' And we do not even know the meaning of difference. 'You don't know the difference until you realize there is no difference—then you know it.' More subtle still, he tells the story of the Emperor who, faced with a Zen master, thought he understood that he was in fact the Buddha. But the master made it clear that the Emperor and the Buddha 'are not *two* identical things but two *identical* things.'

The higher we climb the more we make friends with nonsense, the more we laugh, at every thing and every person, most of all ourselves. For we laugh when we no longer fear; when self is gone who fears, or could be afraid of what? The Spirit is light and the earth is heavy; the more of Spirit the less of the weight of seriousness to hold us down. Some are shocked on visiting the Buddhist Society to find us laughing merrily; the English Puritan tradition of religious gloom dies hard. 'Zen', says Blyth, 'has in it a kind of gusto, a kind of energy which shines forth in the smallest thing.' But is there small or great? The self must writhe in bondage; the Spirit is free—to laugh.

All possessions are forms of fear, lest we lose them. As we cease to possess then we can safely cease to fear. Indeed there is 'nothing special' as the Zen men say, in all that we have and do and are. Let us move through life 'leaving no trace', no causes which will need our presence for their due effect. We can afford now to be ignorant, for knowledge is a burden we no longer need. And we shall be humble, remembering the tremendous statement in the *Tao Te Ching*, 'Be humble, and you will remain entire.' The operative word is remain. Where ego does not raise its head, what is there to be knocked off, as an excrescence on the smooth sphere of Reality? The braggart self which, knowing its unimportance thinks with large desires to bring the greatest possible ambit of its circumstance to full obedience, is seen for what it is, an outworn, troublesome illusion. How pleasant when the balloon of self subsides and the mind may rise to visions of the infinite, and further still, to learn that 'there is nothing infinite apart from finite things' and 'to do finite things in an infinite way'. Do we now see how 'the whole is the whole, but the part is infinite'; see that large and small are complementary adjectives without true meaning, that time and space, the Ultimate and the job in hand are all utterly and happily here and now?

As vision comes, as we loosen the mind's restrictions, as the working mind is more and more illumined with the light of Buddha-Mind we feel a foretaste of serenity, that 'constant and unwavering steadiness of heart upon the arrival of every event, whether favourable or unfavourable', as the Bhagavad Gita has it; of certainty, as more and more we *know*; of 'the joy that cometh in the morning' beyond the sway of change, and suffering, and the pursuit of a Nirvana already attained.

And as we cross the Bridge that is not, we find our wakening Wisdom functioning in a thousand helpful forms as deep Compassion for all people, things and circumstance, not always least, ourselves.

19

Phase Four: Beyond Thought

Let us repeat here the Caption in the Syllabus:

As the ceiling of Samsara, the dual world of unreality, is pierced with the sword of Prajna-intuition, allowing 'peeps' of a wider state of consciousness, we reach the true beginning of Zen training. Each experience is incommunicable in words but each has the common factor that self has disappeared. These are 'moments of awareness', not of my awareness of some thing which was not there before. Here subject/object, past, present and future, you and I no longer exist in separation. We now see everything as it is, and all things as inseverable parts of the same Fullness/Emptiness. This is the true beginning of Zen training which Dr Suzuki called 'a moral training based on the experience of Satori'.

We approached the Bridge and saw that there could not be a bridge between duality and Non-duality, mind and No-Mind, the relative of here and now and the Absolute. We saw further, that none is needed for the two are one.

We began to see with the intuition, which supersedes all reason, logic and much sense. We accepted the irrational, the non-sense of life as it really is and laughed happily. We made bold use of thought to control the process of thought, and used thought-forces as chosen to raise habitual thought to the level of Illumined Thought. We are nearer now to the readiness which is the prelude to enlightenment. Truly, 'the readiness is all'.

What now? We have seen that we cannot command the experience of Satori, nor the least peep of it. We can but look and wait. While waiting we should look at what we want, and why. For motive is now more vital still. Not merely because with wrong motive we shall certainly misuse the tremendous force of enlightenment when it comes, but any motive at all implies an 'I' that is fighting for what it wants. And this is fatal to success.

Why? The answer lies in two more concepts, blinding truths to those who suddenly 'see'. We must face them. So far I, a being with a will to attain enlightenment, have sought it strenuously in a course which is a condensed description of a process taking many lives.

No such being attains enlightenment, first because there is no such being, and secondly because, to the extent that there is, there is nothing for such being to attain.

The first proposition is, as we have seen, the very heart's core of the Diamond Sutra, as of the Heart Sutra which we recite together in Class. 'From the first not a thing is', as we noted in the chapter on the Wisdom gone Beyond, and in all that is, Unborn and born, there are no beings. All alike are 'falsely imagined'.

The second proposition, conceding an ever-changing being as an appearance in the world of duality, states that such a being will never attain Enlightenment for there is no enlightenment to attain. All such beings are already enlightened. Once again we quote *The Voice of the Silence*, 'Look within, thou art Buddha.' And Huang Po, 'All the Buddhas and all sentient beings are nothing but the One Mind, besides which nothing exists.' Both these propositions are equally true. As someone nobly put it, the Buddha in his Wisdom saw there were no beings, and with his Compassion worked to save them.

Then what are we doing here, in Class or reading of it, we that do not exist striving to attain what we have? The answer can only be given, if at all, in terms of paradox. In easier language, however, we must drop the self-wound bandage from our eyes, 'be naked to experience' and see with increasing clarity our own Divinity.

But here is a third and final thought, that it is not I that seek enlightenment. As Father Merton wrote in his amazing work, *Mystics and Zen Masters*, and I make no apology for quoting yet again, 'Zen insight is not our awareness, but Being's awareness of itself in us.' This is the supreme discovery of the mystic and in the moment that we know it to be true we are reborn.

In this one phrase is half the scriptures of the world. Why did God create the universe? To know Himself as God. As each and every spark of the parent Flame reaches the state of allowing the One Light to merge within that tiny flame, so the Light is that much brighter, God just so much nearer to awareness that He is Absolute, and God.

With some dim vision of this supernal truth it is easier to understand how every moment of enlightenment is a little death, a wound in the body of self, a further deflation of the ego, which is born of the illusion that any separate, distinct, abiding self was ever born or ever could be. We can now merge the two basic terms in our enquiry, Zen and Enlightenment, for we see that Enlightenment is sudden awareness of Zen, Zen being no less than the Light of the Unborn in manifestation.

What then is Satori, a first awareness of Zen? Says Dr Suzuki, 'the life of Zen begins with the opening of Satori', and 'the object of Zen discipline is to prepare our relative consciousness for it.' This course is concerned with that preparation. For each of us it means 'the unfolding of a new world hitherto unperceived in the confusion of a dualistic mind'. Note that it is the beginning of Zen training, not the end. We have broken out of the chrysalis of self into the field of universality. As Dr Suzuki says in a quotation I cannot trace, 'Enlightenment is not a mere personal affair which does not concern the community at large; its background is laid in the universe itself.' He adds, of interest to all of us who feel impatient, 'it requires a long preparation, not of one life but of many lives'.

What is it like? Note the form of the question, which is answerable; to ask what it *is* is quite unanswerable. For description implies the use of concepts, themselves the wrought products of thinking in a field of duality. Satori is beyond conception, beyond duality. Dr Suzuki puts it firmly: 'if Satori is amenable to analysis in the sense that by so doing it becomes perfectly clear to another who has never had it, that satori will be no satori. A satori turned into a concept ceases to be itself, and there will be no more a Zen experience.'

Many attempts have nevertheless been made, and the records of the Zen School are full of them. In anthologies like the Mumonkan (the Gateless Gate) and the Hekiganroku (Blue Cliff Records) there are many stories of the 'moment' of enlightenment which came to the questioner at some remark or gesture, even a blow, from the master. In many of his writings Dr Suzuki has given translations of stories from *The Transmission of the Lamp*, and has devoted chapters on the theme of Satori in his *Introduction to Zen Buddhism* and in the First Series of his *Essays in Zen Buddhism*. But whatever be written or said there can be no transmission of the actual experience. As a master said firmly to an imploring pupil, 'I really have nothing to impart to you. Besides, whatever I can tell you is my own and can never be yours.' Even Dr Suzuki's own first satori, as described in *The Field of Zen* is tantalizing in its brevity.

Westerners too have tried to describe their first awakening. Douglas Harding, in *On having no Head*, echoes ingredients of older descriptions.

'It was a revelation at long last of the perfectly obvious. . . . It was all perfectly simple and plain and straight-forward, beyond argument, thought and words. There arose no reference beyond the experience itself, but only peace and a quiet joy, and the sensation of having dropped an intolerable burden.' Others in the Buddhist Society have written of their own experience and one at least remarked that in a world of heightened, sharper vision he noticed that 'the wheels of a cart go round'.

Just as after long treatment for some pain we suddenly notice that the pain has gone, so on our approach to enlightenment we suddenly notice a burden shed, a sense of integration in some universal Plan too vast to visualize, a profound alteration of attitude to life and people, and to the folly of circumstance. We are not aware of going to sleep, or of being asleep, but when we wake we realize how deeply we had been asleep. We wake to the old world newly seen.

There are of course degrees of Satori, and its intensity seems to grow out of the will. 'Zen grows out of the will as the first principle of life,' says Dr Suzuki, and again, 'the will is the man himself and Zen appeals to it.' But each experience, large or, as Hakuin said of the others, 'the little ones that make one dance', is unmistakeable. The beginner, however, must beware of counterfeits. Psychic visions and 'hunches' are not Satori, nor the sudden 'bright idea' which arrives in the course of study. Nor is the trance or ecstasy achieved in the process of Dhyana, and much of the teaching of the sixth Patriarch, Hui-Neng, was dedicated to the distinction between this deep meditation and the awakening of Prajna-intuition. The tests to be self-applied are simple. As Hui-Neng says, 'he who is puffed up by the slightest impression "I am now enlightened" is no better than he was when under delusion'. Would that all Western students had those words illumined over their meditation seat! An experience in which there is still a sense of I is no true Satori.

The experience will slightly fade. Therefore it must be expressed in some way, to clinch it, prove it, 'salt it down'. Hence the practice of interviews in Rinzai Zen, when the master urges the successful one to further efforts and helps him to 'mature' the experience. No effort will produce the next experience, but if the will to apply it to all men be intense enough it seems that a conduit pipe is opened between the infinite Source of the Wisdom/Love and the new means of supplying all with it. The more and wider the 'peeps' the more Enlightenment is made available for all mankind.

One can, I claim, still use the intellect to help achieve the next experience. It is like the fast run up to the high jump or, as Alan Watts once put it in a letter to me about his training with the late Sasaki Roshi, 'Zen involves no discarding of the intellect; it must be developed to the highest pitch, to the point where ultra-rapid reasoning becomes so immediate that the process of reasoning apparently disappears.' Yet the result can be genuine awareness and not mere rapid thought. The distinction remains at all times. So long as there are two things there is no Zen, not even when the two things are the attainable and the Unattainable. As Dr Suzuki wrote in a manuscript not yet published, 'Zen discipline is different from intellectualization. It does not stand away from the Unattainable but plunges right into it and experiences it *as unattainable*.' (Italics mine.)

The results will come when neither sought nor cared for. Not necessarily in the outer man, still bound by his karma and present character. The experience 'is simply an inner state of consciousness without reference to its objective consequences'. Many results have been described. Serenity, a peace in conflict at 'the still centre of the turning world'; a sense of a 'Power divine' working through one to its own supernal ends; a patience to watch the Plan unfold without the interference of approval or disapproval.

There is a sense of self enormously reduced (though even a master may get peevish at his failing memory!). There is now 'nothing special' as the Zen men say, in any thing or happening, no pride of achievement; not the least will to set up as a Saviour of mankind on the strength of some experience. But with the death of fear—for who shall now be afraid of what?—comes laughter, constant care-free laughter at everything and everyone, including most oneself. With laughter comes compassion, an awareness of suffering now seen without emotion, its cause revealed, and a clear vision of the next thing to be done to alleviate such part of it as it seems one's karma will permit.

The movement onward is unceasing. As Dr Suzuki explained when writing of the Samurais' adoption of Zen Buddhism, 'Zen wants to act, and the most effective act is, once the mind is made up, to go on without looking backward.' And the movement is immediate, with no thing allowed to intervene between decision and action. 'Change is inherent in all component things' says the first of the Buddhist Signs of Being. The wise move with it. As the master Ryokwan ended a poem, 'I follow my karma as it moves, with perfect contentment.' The Zen life is thus the quintessence of right action, the Karma yoga of the Bhagavad Gita combined with the passive non-reaction of Taoism.

There is a famous saying in Zen records to the effect that 'usual life is very Tao', or Zen, but this for most of us is a very unusual life. 'What is more wonderful than this, I carry water and fetch fuel?' Yes, but in a mood very different from the ceaseless craving of the ordinary man. From the first moment of enlightenment the newly awakened mind uses distinction and discrimination as before but ceases to note the difference. It learns to engage in life while transcending its triviality. It learns 'the infinite way of doing finite things'. As Blyth once put it, 'we no longer do what we like—we like what we do'. And the will behind the action is Dharma, the next thing to be done. Action becomes smooth and direct. 'When hungry I eat, when tired I sleep.' No fuss now, no anxiety. Dimly yet more clearly we begin to see that Nirvana is indeed Samsara; heaven is here and now. As the poem 'On Trust in the Heart' puts it,

> One in All, All in One—
> If only this were realized
> No more worry about not being perfect.

We need not worry at all, about ourselves or others. 'It is all right.' Four words meaning what they say. Digested at high level, as it were, this tremendous saying makes a profound change in our outer action, expressing the new vision. The Arhat and the Bodhisattva life are fused in unceasing action for the good of all mankind. We have reached and passed through Satori. And learnt? That there is no such thing as Satori. Walk on!

Questions
Ask yourself what question you will but see that you answer it out of Zen experience, no less!

EXPERIMENTS IN ZEN

In the spiritual life no theory is of value unless applied, and the Zen Class is far more than a discussion group. From time to time we have, as it were, spread out our findings, changed beliefs, new points of view on the floor between us, and some fifteen years ago we began the practice of a series of written questions which members took away with them to write me their replies. All were treated as confidential, and in due course I would give back to the Class a résumé of their answers. The results were, at the request of the Class, published in *The Middle Way* in 1967 as 'Experiment in Zen' and are here reproduced as at least one answer to the question often raised, in genuine enquiry or mild abuse, 'What is the good of it all?' or, more plainly put, 'What are the results?'

These articles do not, of course, describe results, in the sense of a record of Zen experience, for a genuine experience can never be described in terms of value to the beginner-mind, but they do describe the ferment of mind engendered by this training, the awakening of intuitive perception, and the general raising of consciousness in preparation for actual experience. Some readers may be helped by even this brief description.

20

Experiment in Zen

My article in the February issue on 'Zen for the West' has produced considerable comment, much of it in the answers to the third of three questions I put to members of the Zen Class. The purpose of the Questions, to be answered not too briefly and in writing, was first, to make the members think clearly about their attitude to Zen and thus to learn much about themselves, and secondly to help me to place them for the coming session in the Beginners' Class or the Zen Class (closed for each Session). Needless to say, a written paper was not the sole means of judgment but it is the only one of which anything may be published. Even the written papers were for my eye alone, but I have found the contents so profoundly interesting that, without breaking any confidence, I have agreed to publish certain extracts and conclusions without delay. For this is the raw material of Western Zen, the unpolished and unedited expression of inner processes and direct experience which will help to decide the future of the Zen movement in Europe.

The three Questions were:

1. *Why have you chosen Zen Buddhism for your study, as distinct from any other school?*
2. *What do you mean by the Zen which you are seeking, and how fiercely are you seeking it? Add, if you wish, the results of your search so far.*
3. *I want your views on the stability of Japanese Zen technique to Zen in the West. If not thought entirely suitable, I want your views on the best way of approaching, practising and teaching Zen in London in the absence of a qualified teacher.*

The results were immensely different, extremely virile and often quite contradictory, exemplifying once again the two main types of the human mind. They cut across all differences of sex, age and education, and the profundity of opinion and experience was not commensurate

L

with the time already spent on the study of Zen. The Questions being interrelated, the answers are often so blended that they overlap, but most of the twenty sets of answers so far received show that a spiritual yeast is working in the mind of the student, with results, pleasant or unpleasant, of illumination, frustration, utter despair, profound joy or merely a growing sense of the oneness of all things. But the yeast is working, and out of it will come, for better or worse, the school of English Zen. I say English, for other European races may take to it differently, even as we in the West may produce a form or vehicle of Zen very different from that of the Japanese. I have used italics to stress the point being made. All italics are mine.

Why Zen Buddhism?

Many students have travelled a long way before they arrived at Buddhism. Christian mysticism, Existentialism, Yoga, Theosophy, Spiritualism, New Thought, Psychology, Comparative Religion, even Catholicism, all had been tried and found wanting. The reasons were as varied as the substitutes rejected, but for many Buddhism was a relief from dogma, ritual and reliance on some Saviour. But why Zen Buddhism? Because the Theravada was not enough, being too limited. 'While Theravada is a cut and dried scientific and intellectual study of Buddhism, Zen is refreshingly revolutionary in its approach. All our upbringing with its conventions, convictions, rules, beliefs and dual thinking is only there to stimulate the ego. We must drop all this, and by means of our very conventions, rules, beliefs and dual thinking.' And another: 'Zen follows on as the next step after Theravada. After analysing all things until there is nothing left, it is essential to transmute that bleak nothingness into something alive; otherwise the intellectual barrenness of Theravada would lead to loss of balance.' And another: 'Any teaching that is developed, spoken and written down hardens and becomes more and more tainted. By the mere observance of such teaching one can never reach Satori. Zen goes beyond the conceptual teaching of Buddhism to the very ground and meaning of the Buddha himself. The oneness of the Buddha was the life of his teaching, and Zen contacts this life and is one with its wholeness.'

Many stress this fact that Zen is whole, and all else partial. As a way it is the path to this unity; when achieved it is it. 'Zen incorporates life as a whole. Zen does not stand apart looking at it, or treating aspects of it. It does not moralize. It does not command, reward or punish. It invades and changes everyday life, giving each single moment its significance, but not disrupting the whole. It needs no intermediaries, it has the wonderfully cleansing effect of a violent thunderstorm. Its exclusion of formalism, its new, simple and direct method forces the mind to be at work continuously. Here seem to be rules made to be broken, methods presented only to be cast aside. Zen says: . . . 'Don't accept, don't believe, don't submit. Break away from all you have ever known, tear it to pieces, then start from the beginning.' And again, 'My previous studies and experience have taught me that to meet the ever-changing NEW one has to meet it on its own terms with a fresh, *unconditioned vulnerability*.' This writer develops this theme later and his phrase opens up new vistas of comparison with new-found Western psychology.

But many reply with vehemence that they *didn't* choose Zen; Zen chose them, and they could not escape if they would, a perpetual echo of the theme of the Hound of Heaven. 'I did not choose Zen. A thirsty man doesn't choose water—he drinks it! Without any need of thinking there comes a response from within which knows—after its own fashion—beyond any need to justify itself to the intellect or to anyone else.' And again, 'Why should I seek that which I have ? I can say with honesty that Zen pursues me all through the day, and even when I neglect to be "mindful" my thoughts wander to the Class, to individuals on the same quest, to a Zen book, and so on.' And this writer speaks later of 'the energy which is ever beating at the final concept'. And a third, 'I didn't choose it; I found it and fell in head first, not understanding a word but having all my views turned upside down. It seemed easier like that, not more comprehensible but somehow allowing for *the reasonableness of the absurd*.' How fascinating is that moment when reason is first bored with its own rationality!

Finally, on this question/answer, the importance of the teacher and ample opportunity of access. As one writes, 'When Dr Suzuki came I understood directly with the heart as well as with the mind—the words were largely superfluous. It didn't matter that I was unable to remember much of his lecture afterwards. There had been a transmission of the Dharma to an infinitesimal degree and I was grateful for the experience.' Others develop this theme, that transmission is direct from a Master, but that a lesser teacher can stimulate the pupil to find Zen for himself— within.

What is Zen ?

Most writers point out that it is impossible to answer this question, and that is true. 'The Tao that can be expressed is not the eternal Tao.' But having said this they deliver themselves of a wide variety of scintillating epigram, paradox, quotation and 'illumined confusion', if I may coin the phrase, which shows remarkable virility of experience. Many refer at once to its humour. 'Laughter is an essential ingredient in its method of work. Every other school of Buddhism is full of woe; yet Zen is founded on the same teachings and still comes up smiling.' It is direct. 'By Zen I mean the intuitive insight into real living as distinct from mere existence. If one could live each moment, then life would be bathed in flame of sunrise.' It must be used. 'Sometimes one feels as if Zen is an extension of oneself waiting to be used, if only one could catch up with it.' Another expands this. 'It is a means, a brush to paint with, a spade to till the earth. It must be used and not sought. If not used it can be a hindrance. We can *imagine* that we understand it, and produce a persistant and tenacious superiority. Apply it and use it and the swollen ego deflates . . . I can't say I'm fiercely seeking it, but I'm trying to use it. I haven't got it, but I'm trying to use it. . . .' This is pure Taoism and equally good Zen, for in use the user and the instrument are one. Another writes, 'I might write, "Zen is the experiencing of the moment without thought", but even as I write Zen has gone, together with the experience and the moment. Nevertheless in flowing with Zen as it flows I am *living life* as opposed to *thinking about living*, as we commonly do in the West'; 'Zen', writes another, 'is a technique by which a man reaches unity by bringing it to life. It brings into unity the whole of life as lived from hour to hour. It leads to purposelessness, spontaneous, fearless living in which one is freed from the tension of "What ought I to do or to be"? It is a bird flying through space which has neither length, breadth, height or depth. It has nothing to teach. . . .' Many speak of the Void, but one coins an excellent phrase. 'Zen is that which makes everything else seem empty.' The most common description is its completeness. 'Not in the sense of something coming to an end,' one writes, 'but in the way that all things are balanced, the feeling that any situation is "just so", with no loose ends or ragged edges but complete in itself as a ball is complete.' But the final word is typical of its writer. 'The simple, honest, no-damn-nonsense of Zen carries its own conviction which brooks no dispute.'

Some deal separately with the results of Zen. 'A softening up of my own self-importance—a sense of inner space,' writes one. 'In the performance of an ordinary task which ordinarily I might chafe at but which is now the only possible thing I could be doing, comes an awareness of its momentary "rightness".' Some results are surprising. 'Zen helps enormously in practical life, giving more common sense in handling mundane matters and people. Whilst Samsara and Nirvana are one they are completely distinct, and I see the meaning of "Render unto Caesar". . . .'

So much for Zen, from which we descend to the practical politics of

Zen for the West

Here there was so much diversity of view that it is difficult fairly to summarize. Generally speaking, there was a middle view about using Japanese technique. A late letter commenting on my article 'Zen for the West' speaks for many. 'I suggest that though Zen is not an art in itself it embraces the greatest art of all, the art of living. As in every art the student must learn techniques and disciplines; he must find a form to canalize his inspiration, and unless he is a genius, he must at first *borrow* forms until he can devise his own. Thus the musician will listen to music of other times and places, and will begin by writing music in the manner of the masters. The writer will read all he can, and his first attempts will be modelled on work that has stood the test of time; only when he has mastered certain techniques and learned the rules, can he afford to break those rules and formulate his own. So with Zen; here we have no pattern but that set by the East, and we must learn it and practise it with diligence, until such time as a creative artist appears in this art so strange to us, and formulates a technique more akin to our way of life. It cannot be forced—if Zen is *here*, as I believe, the art-form will arise naturally in the fullness of time. Be patient, my masters.'

On the use of the koan there is much debate. Some say it is the life of Rinzai Zen; others that it is folly to attempt it in the absence of a master. One points out that daily life is full of koans and we have to solve them anyway. All agree on the need for more and more meditation, for whatever the methods used each in the end must 'go it alone'. But several agree that this is a dangerous business. 'Passionate conflicts, desperate confusions and the like are inevitable. It is here that the authority and accessibility of the teacher are vital. He can help the student to understand that these things are mind-made and can be destroyed by the mind which made them.' Several stress that, 'we are brought up in a climate of thought so different from that of the East that we are totally unprepared for its anarchism unless we have first made acquaintance with the Dharma proper'. No student, thinks this writer, 'should be accepted in a Zen class unless he has belonged to the Society for at least a year, attending other lectures or meetings, or can *prove* that he has acquired a good grounding in Buddhism. He must learn discrimination in the Buddhist sense before he is told to reject it. In the West we live amid discriminations, and the ability to make a wise choice must be developed before the student can be safely told that there is no problem, no right and wrong, and that spontaneity is all. Shock tactics are splendid so long as the audience have built up some orthodox strength beforehand. . . .' But the process is individual, and many agree that for it we need more silence, more week-end retreats, with less book-learning and more 'mindfulness'.

We must avoid, say many, the stereotyped formula, of words or action, and be perpetually new. 'The freshness of any discovery, phrase or word becomes stale with repetition, but if new words, new phraseology is demanded, deeper implications and discovery follow as the thing is viewed anew.' But we must be intellectual before we can pass beyond the intellect; we must learn to think before we achieve No-thought.

Whether we use the fierceness of Rinzai Zen or the passivity of Soto Zen, which no doubt equally leads to the Goal, is a matter of opinion in which the writers inevitably divide out into the complementary types of mind. One, typical of others, writes, 'We don't want additional knowledge—we want to "undress" until there is nothing left but the Buddha-nature. And this for me can only be achieved by the shock-treatment of Zen—the direct approach.' Others entirely disagree. 'We come to realize that the only thing to do is let go, to give up.' We need patience, they say, not violence. The answer, of course, is a middle way, and perhaps one of our wisest members may have the last word. 'It would be better for Zen in the West to work out its own technique. This it appears to be doing. . . .'

Such are a few spoonfuls from the cauldron of the Zen Class of the Society. It is bubbling mightily. There will be scum to remove, steam to let off, but this is the spirit moving, in its own time and in its own way. No short cuts are attempted, no tricks allowed. Whether we reach any Goal is beside the point. We are past such folly as seeking one. But at least, while awaiting further assistance, advice or rebuke, we are fiercely, mightily, Zennishly alive.

21

Further Experiment in Zen

In 'Experiment in Zen' I said that the cauldron of the Zen Class of the Society was bubbling mightily. It has now bubbled over into a further experiment, in the group consideration of individual problems, with no apologies to similar experiments in the field of psychology. Meanwhile, as the previous article only reported about half the answers to the first question paper, and as the remainder were if anything of a higher standard still, I have prepared a résumé of views for further comment. The keynote is still the intense virility of personal experience, with the authority of scriptures and well-worn phrases, and all 'isms, even Buddh-ism, left behind. I warned the class of the occult law by which any planned and sustained effort to take the 'shadow' self in hand and to expand consciousness ahead of the average of one's friends and associates, produces its own fresh crop of *dukkha* (suffering), on the mental, emotional and even physical planes. And the troubles came, so thick and fast that I was glad that the sufferers were duly warned. There is indeed a need, as one writer puts it, 'to grade the Class in respect of the teaching given and the exercises demanded with some kind of appraisal of psychological maturity'. But the suffering will be felt, whatever the grade, until the end of self. As the same writer elsewhere says, 'Only by dying to myself in the moment, to words, thought, and even to the desire to die, can Zen be revealed. Only then is the actor and the action one, and the problem and the solution the same.' For the material of the Zen search is life itself. The secret lies 'in accepting life as it presents itself'. Again, 'the task of being alive is to live. To contemplate the futility of it all, and the suffering of it all, thus severing oneself from life, seems to me still a form of escape.' The same happy mind goes further, 'Zen is my way, and I shall go it because I cannot go any other. Besides, I like it. I do not have a goal to which to strive, but simply enjoy walking ... the movement of the walking on is joy.' And as another points out, and psychologists would heartily agree, the walk is with the whole man. 'Because man strives to be whole he is not', and we cannot leave the part of ourselves we loathe and despise at the foot of the hill while the 'better Self' climbs to the top. 'When illumination comes it illumines all of us', and, as another says, 'the goal and the way cannot be different; one finds the way by treading it, one's spiritual forces by using them, and without humility and poverty one gets nowhere at all'. 'Zen', says another, 'is in the living of the moment; it is not to be found anywhere, but comes from an unfolding centre.' Or, as yet another writes, 'the experience of Zen is within this life. Zen is here, not a state to be sought outside life. Religious activity is activity on the plane of daily life', which another caps magnificently with, 'I regard Zen as the religion to abolish all religion. The word religion means a rebinding . . . but Zen, at the supreme moment, swallows itself.'

Of the Zen in the West, these later writers emphasize the need of understanding Zen as it is before seeking to reclothe it; 'else we are in danger of confusing the clothes with Zen, the finger with the moon'. As a woman writer shrewdly points out, we have been supplied with Zen literature for years and yet are still saying 'Give us Zen'. 'We must beware of adding another technique to our collection, and choose between the technique and Zen, which laughs at all systems and teaching.' Most, however, agree that for a time we must have a qualified Roshi to help us, though in the end we must produce our own. Meanwhile, Zen scriptures will help, backed by an indomitable will which in the end will create and use the necessary means.

Such was the position at Easter. From then until June the Society was favoured with the successive presence of three men well known in the world of Zen. Dr Hisamatsu, a lay Roshi and expert on Japanese art, though hampered by the need of translation in what he said, showed us what a Roshi can be. Alan Watts, now a well-known writer and speaker in Zen Buddhism, showed us the thoughts of one of the leading minds in Western Zen; then came Dr Suzuki himself, a man who, having attained his own Zen enlightenment, has spent just sixty years offering it to the West. Yet, as one student wrote, 'the Masters can but give us encouragement, tell us when we are getting warm, and confirm our arrival. No Master has ever claimed more than this.' Dr Suzuki, apparently impressed with the strenuous efforts of the Class to find Zen and to accept no substitutes, has promised to persuade one or more Japanese but English-speaking Roshis to spend substantial time in Europe in the near future. Meanwhile I gave the members a new set of Questions.

1. *How does Zen, or your search for Zen, affect your daily life—your thinking, feeling, reactions, values, motives, acts?*
2. *How in meditation do you attempt to pass the pairs of opposites which are inherent in all thought, and so achieve direct experience of non-duality?*
3. *How do you understand the passive acceptance of all conditions and events, and how do you collate this with the effort or energy which it seems necessary to use in order to achieve any progress or 'experience'?*

The answers were not always given seriatim as in an examination paper, and many members regarded all three as nine-pins to be knocked flat with tremendous gusto. One must be quoted at length, for it was long before I picked myself up off the floor. 'If the search for Zen affects one's outlook vastly, it probably means that one was not really of a suitable make-up for this particular path. A tree does not search for its fruits, it grows them. So should one's pursuit of Zen be the result of one's attitude to life, and not be regarded as a new line to follow. It is useless for a pear tree to desire apples. Thus I do not use Zen practices to reform myself but to express myself.' And that's that.

Others, less fiercely direct, talk of the 'horrible little self' which must be faced, admitted to exist, and included in the total 'Self' which is advancing. For them 'Zen creates a background against which thoughts, feelings and personal troubles are seen as forms of limitation'. Or to use another analogy, 'Everything seems like parts of one big picture, each part being as important, or not important, as each other'. But the great discovery of many members is the direct approach to things as they are. 'Whatever the matter to be done, it is approached on its own level, with eager friendliness accepted in its own right and carried through with the fullest attention and devotion one can give. One rises to the situation, assimilates it, lives in it, and the action gets accomplished so'. When youth is thus on the right lines what will its owner not accomplish in age? 'We must learn to live in the present', says another, 'but there must be "more looking".' 'I live more intensely', writes another, 'while I think and therefore worry less.' And the 'looking' or objective examination of all things and events may be and should be carried out, not with a wary eye on *dukkha* (suffering), but with *joie de vivre*, the 'spontaneous knowledge of a dynamic livingness'. 'How absurd it is to drag the past into the present, so beautifully alive.' 'My search for Zen has chiefly brought me joy', writes another, and this is sharply distinguished from the pleasures of the senses. 'Other people are taken more for what they are than what I want them to be', writes one who has not heard of Jungian 'withdrawal of projections' but is doing it. And this withdrawal produces a greater independence of external factors, a greater detachment from events, a loosening of ties, 'detachment as distinct from indifference'. 'I have at long last really seen the point of depending only on oneself—the wonderful release in abandoning all hope.' Applying the same discovery another says, 'As I see it, the Zen Buddhist observes the code of conventional morality not because he considers it to have any intrinsic value but because the reasons which might impel the ordinary person to break it do not operate in his case', which is to many of us an utterly new idea.

Several have found their way to the mighty saying, 'All that happens happens right', one member by loosening the hold of the dichotomy of like and dislike, which is coupled, the writer finds, with an increasing respect for other people, 'unaffected by the fact that their acts, emotions and ideas may be at complete variance with one's own. Life is truly one.' For this member, tragedy has lost its value—'for what can go wrong?' Just 'allow things to happen. Zen says get out of the way, and the effort one has to make is just to get out of the way'. With all this new awareness comes a new understanding of compassion, as the necessary fruits of the oneness of life. One writes of 'the suffering of others about which I can do nothing that causes me intense anguish of spirit'. Another could help her, with his analysis of all sense of suffering into concepts which can with effort be discarded. Regret for the past and anxiety about the future are alike thought-forms, ensouled with imagination. But this is itself of the intellect and the heart still suffers, and must suffer until of each burning human tear it may be said 'thyself hast wiped it from the sufferer's eye'. Only the mind in Prajna can cease from such reaction, and the Bodhisattva heart does not choose to do so.

For asking Question 2 I was rebuked by the same writer who dealt so pungently with Question 1. 'I do not regard the pairs of opposites as parallel lines which can never meet. I realize that in passing beyond them I bring them with me in another form. Were I to reject the opposites I should simply create a new pair, duality versus non-duality. So to achieve the experience of non-duality I must cease to concern myself with it as such, because it is impossible to "regard" anything in a non-dualistic manner. Therefore I attempt to lose all sense of "regarding".' With some writers I should be tempted to consider this slick intellectuality. Here, it is, I think, genuine experience. Many others speak of the watching, or regarding or steady looking at things, and this is common ground to many schools of Buddhism. One describes it as in the field of psychology. 'I have become aware of this search [for Zen] as if it were a dance between the inner and outer life. One just sits and watches, and magic things stir in the dark waters preparatory to rising to the surface. What forms they will take I do not know, but they live and have strong powers of movement and vitality.' This increasingly objective attitude to mental happenings is all to the good, for it develops the power to withdraw projections, on which Jung lays so much stress, and restores the integrity of the 'whole man' who must use the 'one-moment' of timelessness for every act. Some tackle the opposites from the top, that is, from the concept of that in which they are subsumed and merged in one (while remaining two). 'I start with an attempt to drop "self", and then try to concentrate on the theme from the top of the triangle. Then other "thoughts" come through, as though released, but they are not "thoughts".' But as another points out, the experience of 'non-duality has nothing to do with thinking, and we must simply let the truth of this operate'. It operates 'by relieving one of a host of concepts. We are free to pay attention to the task in front of us. Walking is walking and eating is eating. . . .' (Thus are famous Zen phrases reborn in Western minds in the crucible of experience.)

I will close this section by quoting an experience which calls for no comment. 'I started on the opposites without knowing it by following the instructions in *The Cloud of Unknowing*. I said one short word, God, and repeated it until my mind was saying it in rhythm with my breathing, 23 hours a day, non-stop. This created an acute tension, and I could not distinguish between God and the Devil. This produced an awful despair. I felt I was too evil to recognize goodness. . . . Still the Hound pursued, and the tension grew. Then I came home—to Zen. I meditated on the opposites. As any thought came to me I pushed it into the unconscious and left the whole lot to simmer. Then one day it all boiled over and took possession of me. I went round with a certainty that I was going mad, muttering to myself "Nirvana and Samsara, they are one". Then one afternoon in Kensington Gardens I gave up. I sat looking at the flowers, completely exhausted. Gradually I was aware of an all-pervading calm, pouring in. At last I was at peace and the Hound no longer pursued. I know that I know, but what I know I do not know.'

About passivity in action or effort-less energy the battle raged merrily. Most were agreed on the necessity of cultivating acceptance, of circumstances outside and also within the mind. Many invoked the law of Karma. 'I have never willingly lain down under adversity, but I have learned the wisdom of inner acceptance through my faith in the law of Karma. My (very Western) instinct is to take immediate action, but I sometimes find acceptance itself to be a form of action.' And another: 'the passive acceptance of all conditions and events is absolutely necessary, for they are our karmic balance carried forward from our previous births'. Some find the effort to accept considerable. 'Sustained effort is needed to break through the layers with which we have surrounded Reality, and this energy is in no way affected by acceptance of present conditions.' Another puts this negatively. 'Passivity in my case means throwing off compulsions and inhibitions', but the throwing off is a form of effort. Effort is truly necessary, and we must accept, as one puts it, the necessity of effort! Perhaps acceptance comes first. 'If I wish to drop a particular habit I must just drop it; it is useless to get involved with self-reproaches, resolutions and moralizing, a method which resembles one's attempt to get rid of a sticky piece of paper. . . .' So the writers get closer and closer to the resolution of the tension. One sees the pair as pull and push. 'Thus Absolute pulls the relative particle as a magnet an iron filing; the filing pushes to reach the Absolute.' Another gets nearer still. 'I don't see the problem here. You see a problem only if you think energy can't operate without a conscious object to strive towards. But attachment only dissipates energy. . . .' (I think of Suzuki's 'The strength of no desire.') Yet another is perhaps nearer still. 'Passive acceptance is only a fact when I stand face to face with a fact accepting it for what is it, without excusing it or trying to change it. It is what it is—in that point-instant of the moment. . . . The clarity of perception which enables one to face a fact or situation with all one's attention manifests one's dynamism, effort or energy, and one's action is but the unimpeded continuity with which the situation is dealt with. . . .'

These are but sayings and thoughts collected from some 30 papers averaging 300 words. Some are finding the pace too hot for them; they are resting and may renew the battle later. But others, so far from being pursued by the Hound of Heaven are in full cry after the Hound and yelping with happy excitement. What a Master would think of it all I know not, but I think he would smile, and the smile would be full of Zen.

22

Third Experiment in Zen

Nature proceeds by jumps and pauses, seldom by the 'steady progress' beloved by chairmen of City Companies, and the answers to the third set of Questions were in the main uninspired. The first two were:

> What is the relation between your present inner self-development and the awakening of Bodhi-citta, compassion for all forms of life and their suffering?

> 'Usual life is very Tao (or Zen).' Interpreted superficially this is a dangerous half-truth; deeply understood it might become the foundation of Western Zen. What is your understanding?

A fourth set of Questions covered the ground of the above two but went deeper. The results were fascinating, and produced the finest display of intuitive flashes yet achieved. The Questions were:

1. *Karma has been called the law of harmony, and breaches of the law produce effects on the breaker. Compassion has been called 'the Law of Laws, eternal Harmony'. Can you 'see' that Karma and Compassion are truly aspects of one law of Harmony? If so, show me that you 'see'.*
2. *'Every-day mind is Zen.' 'Usual life is very Tao.' 'It's here, in the dustbin.' All true, but how true to you? Show me.*
3. *'Be humble and remain entire.' This is a quotation in the* Tao Te Ching, *which shows it is old indeed, perhaps one of the oldest truths in the hearts of men. How true is it to you?*

The Class has now reached the stage when individual development, and the great variety of roads along which it is achieved, produce a complexity of 'level' and method of approach which, in a body of thirty citizens may well be an epitome of the Western mind. Types have become clear-cut, the natural mystic, the intuitive-intellectual, the philosophic-ritualist, the Taoist gardener, the extroverted, self-analysing psychologist, and a dozen more, most of them remarkably tolerant, in a deep sense, of each other's profoundly different line of approach to the same Reality. But in each member the distinctions between hit and miss, often seen by the writer answering the questions, are equally apparent. One writes 1,200 words on the first Question, producing a first class article on the subject, but heavily intellectual, and then in a dozen lines for Question 2 hits, as it were, the ceiling with intuitive awareness. The speed of reaction is so different as to be embarrassing. Some of the best Answers come through the post in a few days; others complain at the end of two months that they are still 'simmering' and the answer has not yet 'come through'. But all have a deeper sense of integration, with Life, with circumstance, with each other and all that lives. One, for example, after a class at which we had discussed the 'closing of the gap' between Nirvana and Samsara, wrote a sudden postcard in the middle of the morning's household chores: 'What waste of time sweating away to close the gap that isn't there! Our distress comes from trying to pull the one apart and make it two, and it won't budge. No wonder we get a bit tired?'

It will be convenient to consider together No. 1 of the third set of Questions, on compassion, and No. 1 on the fourth set on compassion, harmony and Karma.

These concepts, and the deep religious and spiritual realities they symbolize, were found so interlinked that it was evidence of an incipient and growing awareness of their basic unity. Most took as their basic concept, Harmony. 'The universe is one and indivisible. Hence the law of Harmony governs it. Everybody and everything influences every other thing and every other body, and is in turn influenced by them. A polar bear coughs at the North Pole and the sands of the Sahara stir. There is no separate self. Cosmic energy is not divided into individual persons. Compassion is the outcome of this knowledge. . . .' And again, 'Life is stark real, vitally alive and so closely interwoven that no distinction is possible. All is an inside-outside relationship, all equally part of my set-up, and in daily life one sets off every moment a new chain-reaction. It is breath-taking. I watch and react and become and change and flow . . . inside-outside, where is the border?' From this unceasing 'changing, merging, altering, being born and dying, each ephemeral object's Karma is its potential, its innermost becoming manifest in space-time. Thus myriads of potentials of Karma stream out from one in all directions to embrace the whole universe. Viewing one man's life, his Karma gives it homogeneity, forms it into a living whole so that his past lives on with him.'

Another takes it up; 'The deepening understanding of the oneness of life produces an equally growing compassion for all forms of life. Then the stone is my brother. . . . But I must have experienced it *myself*. Only then is my compassion a reflex-action at one with life, and has the warmth of it, and the "whole-making" effect. If it is self-motivated, even with the best motives, it causes results, hence Karma.' Here enters self. 'It is our own sick-mindedness that prevents us having a natural spontaneous compassion for other people.' And again, 'We become aware of Karmic laws only when we stop becoming objective in our attitude to life. Only a sense of "I" can interfere with Harmony, for Harmony is undivided and it is the sense of "I" which divides. The awareness of Karma shows we are off-balance, as the Law is only felt in dualism. We are unaware of Compassion; when we are aware of it, it is not compassion.' To see dually, several conclude, is due to the Karma created by disturbance of the Harmony which only Compassion, spontaneously arising, can restore. 'When we are out of step with the oneness, Karma is required to restore the balance.'

But we must be aware of the break, the disturbance, before we can cure it; else we are merely pushed about by the Law. 'To rise one must start at the bottom. There must be a known break before making whole.' 'The laws of Karma are our teachers if we can recognize Compassion at work beneath them.' 'Compassion', writes another, 'is the constant, conscious desire to bless anyone anywhere, as they touch our consciousness. In this I fulfil my own law of Harmony, or pay the price for not so doing.'

Another writes, 'I see both Karma and Compassion as the "skilful means" of one law of Harmony, two brooms both sweeping the path that leads to Harmony'. But here comes a gentle reproof for talking about 'laws', lest we imagine a law-giver. 'It is not that Karma exists and we fit into it, but Karma is the word we use to describe our actions and reactions.' That is well said. Several imported suffering as the factor common to these concepts. 'Only the acceptance of one's own suffering leads to a willingness to share in the suffering of others', writes one, and another may mean the same thing when he asks that we spare a little time to be sorry for ourselves. For it is the self that causes all the trouble. Adds another, 'What a paradox it is that to drop the self one must first experience it, live with it, examine it; these feelings of pride, fear and the like dissolve not by being rejected but by being lived with'. Thus is Karuna born. It cannot be aroused deliberately though we can and should act 'as if', by living 'as if' the flame were already awake. But because 'Compassion can only manifest itself unselfconsciously, a compassionate man would be in a sense unaware that it had arisen in him'. Hence the truly compassionate act is spontaneous, without thought before or recollection afterwards. For as another wrote, 'After years of wringing my heart with sympathy for others' suffering I realize that this is no true compassion but a form of self-indulgence'. The ideal, thinks another, is to act naturally, natural to the mind that has ceased to see people as separate entities and knows them now as One.

So 'the debate continues'—about a general concept of the Universe as in Harmony, with self-full actions breaking that Harmony, to the debit of the one who broke it. Compassion is seen as the healing force which makes *one* where the disturbance of the equilibrium and oneness had made two, the healing or 'whole-ing' power to offset the destructive force of our folly.

Question 2. From struggling in the coils of these tremendous principles the Class turned to the more extrovert conception of 'usual life' or 'everyday mind' as 'Tao' or 'Zen'. The danger referred to in the original question is very real. It is far too easy to assume that 'ordinary life' lived in the full measure of habitual fatuity will in some way one day produce enlightenment. This was far from the purpose of the creator of the original phrase. In the nineteenth item in the *Mumonkan* we read, 'Nansen was asked by Joshu, "What is Tao?" Nansen answered, "Ordinary mind is Tao." "Should we try to get it?" asked Joshu. "As soon as you try you miss it," was the master's reply.' The point, as most writers discovered, is in Suzuki's words, 'There is nothing infinite apart from finite things', or as a member put it, 'This and here and now is the field of experience. If we run to the farthest ends of the world we cannot escape from ordinary life. Where else can we go for Enlightenment?' Therefore, 'relax into life as it comes', says another, 'not living for the special occasions and disregarding what goes between. Let daily life just be; do every little thing whole-heartedly and relinquish it without regret when done.' As to what mind to use, 'what other mind have I but my everyday mind?' asks one. 'Only a hypocrite has a Sunday mind. Zen is whole, all, everything, in what one finds as in what one rejects of pain, humility and daily work.' All this is obvious, writes another, 'so obvious that how can I *show* you my understanding? Can one describe the state of water?' What is needed, many agree, is 'an unusual way of living usual life'. To live in the moment is the secret, find several. 'But living in the now is an impossibility without giving up the desire for past and future, and a willingness to accept the now whether nice or nasty.' The trouble as ever is the self. 'It simply cannot bear to be left out of anything.' But need it be? 'Life in the Tao-way is pure action within the "moment". No thinking, no speculating before, during or after the act. The act fills up the whole of the moment. . . . If we could live thus all the time we should be enlightened.' The violent effort to see in the ash-tray the whole universe is waste of time. It is there, but so long as there is a seer and a seen, there are two things, and the truly "usual" life is lived in non-duality. For Zen is freedom, and only the free man, made free by Prajna, can live the purposeless life of Zen which, seeing no distinctions, or seeing them as the mind-born children of illusion, is equally content with a dustbin or a symphony, sewing on a button or trying on a crown. All this implies struggle, say many. 'It is all an intense struggle, but this struggle is quite useless and leads nowhere. Yet without it the next stage would never happen. This is when the struggle is given up, and until this happens there can be no enlightenment.' But Zen, says another, 'releases the energy once wasted in dealing with the confusion of the relative world. Am I on the right path? Am I doing the right thing? Zen is confident and free from anxiety.' 'It is when we "drop it" that we *know* . . . Zen is unknowable, indescribable, but it works.' Thus the *Tao Te Ching* has the last word. 'When one looks at it one cannot see it. When one listens to it one cannot hear it. But when one uses it it is inexhaustible.' Applying this, a new member preferred to express herself in verse:

> As I make my every day,
> I look upon people, places, things,
> Label them good or bad, high or low,
> Mine and thine.
> And thus divided, they confuse me.

> But when as an arrow
> Loosed by It
> I touch the Centreless Centre,
> Where to put a dustbin—
>   Or yet a diamond—
>   Or even me?

> After that, in usual life,
> When a mudbank or a star I see,
> I smile,
> And let it be.

Question 3. 'Be humble and you will remain entire.' I have long been fascinated by the fact that this phrase was thought so great that it is actually quoted in the *Tao Te Ching*, itself one of the greatest Scriptures in the world. Many members in my view missed the grandeur entirely, and reduced it to a trite admonition against personal conceit. Some even objected to the word humility as smacking of humiliation. The individual must assert himself at times, else he remains one of the herd—and so on. A few got near to the heart of the tremendous statement by grasping the word 'remain', and some of these appreciated that 'it is a state of mind directly conditioned by the heart'. Or, as another put it, 'This is the heart of the matter but it must not be separated from the head, for in Zen there cannot be two ways. The pilgrims walk on this or other paths, yet there is only one pilgrim and he must become the Path to tread it.' But we must *remain* entire, 'and not cut off the bit of us we don't like. We must accept our Wholeness.' As another wrote, 'I must step down to step up', which reminds me of my favourite saying of a pupil long ago, 'Before we can become extraordinary we must learn to become extra ordinary!' The facet of acceptance was much to the fore. 'To live life humbly is not to make demands of it, not to reproach it, to ask no more than the present moment brings.' We must be content to be nothing as such. 'You are the froth and the foam on the waves of the sea. Let the froth dissolve into the wave, and make the relaxing, expanding, interior gesture towards the freedom of the total sea.' 'No man', wrote another, 'is greater than his power to humble himself.' The secret is to remain in this entirety. Yet another is, I think nearer the mark still. 'The clue is in the word remain. Entirety does not come after being humble. The entirety of being humble is the absence of concern over an "I".' But self has many meanings. As another put it, 'To be humble is to remain with oneself. Not to journey outwards in search of treasure, but to search in one's own cupboard for the widow's mite. Humility knows no fear; for loss and gain are of no account to it. The humble man neither gives nor takes hostages in a war with fortune; he remains simple and unconfused. One cannot decide to be humble. Humility is a by-product of Self-knowledge.'

To the answers to this question I would add a word of my own. In meditation I have begun the other end, with the word 'entire'. Here is the primordial Absolute, one's 'original Face before one was born'. This should never be lost, for it is in the littlest act of the daily round, and never ceases to be. To assert self is to break this harmony, unity, wholeness. Karma steps in to regulate the return to Harmony, to persuade one of the wisdom of remaining entire. This wisdom we call humbleness, non self-assertion. By it we *remain—entire*.

So much for a brief review of the answers to these two sets of Questions, in which I trust that I have not lost the light of intuition which made so many of them worth while. At least it is a record of experience, and if I may end with the words of one of the students on this theme, 'From birth to death all one has is one's experience. This goes on whether one names it or not. Experience is an individual matter, and can only be known as it becomes conscious of its flow, for to name an experience is to give to a passing flow the semblance of fixity. But the world seen as a conglomeration of fixed entities is an illusion, and the attempt to hang on to the flow is where suffering arises. Emptiness being form and form being emptiness, life arises out of the void at each "moment", or between each two "moments", and each of these two gaps is the Void of eternity. To this supreme experience I have not yet come, but from this side of that experience I can hear it in a half-comprehending silence.' It is in the silence that we shall know.

23

Fourth Experiment in Zen

These Questions are designed as being beyond mere doctrine and yet short of the koan, and are aimed at stimulating thought to a point beyond thought, where a true answer may come direct from the intuition. In our class language, I ask for 'Pop-outs', that is, an intuitive answer which just pops out of the mind, whether or not it makes sense, even to the mind concerned.

Here, at the request of the Class, is a fourth summary, for no answer is ever divulged to any other member, and this is one way in which the Class as a whole may learn what is happening in its collective mind.

Question 1. We all know that the 'lower self' which fights for its own advantages is unreal, untrue and an illusion. Who or what knows this?

The proportion of truly intuitive, as distinct from wrought-from-thinking replies, is perhaps slightly improving. There is still a need, however, for more 'pop-outs' and less midnight oil!

Some flatly rejected the statement of duality implied in the Question. 'Who says that the lower self is lower? Why not up-end it to say that the top is filthy and the bottom clean?' 'The Battle of the selves', writes another, 'is an illusion, because in fact it is only the little self having a civil war—the opposites forever negating one another. . . . Let the battle rage of itself!' Others admit the struggle but regard it as illusion.

> The 'lower self' and the 'higher self'!
> Why does the Honourable One make rude noises?
> Still seeking the dog's Buddha Nature?
> The truth is plain to see. Look! Look!

Others accept a 'Higher Third' above the combatants, which sees the True and Untrue and consumes their duality. Some refer to this as 'our Original Face', or 'the Buddha within'. Another asks, 'Why does man have to know what he is not? (The answer is because) God comes out of Himself to know Himself as Self and not-Self. So man has to know what he is not that he may know what he is.' Another gives a later stage of the process. 'When the corn has been through the winnowing machine—it knows.' Some attacked the very word know. 'Knowing is the ever-fresh experience that surprises the eternal moment anew each time. . . . It is an ever present attitude of mind.' Another keeps his feet well on the ground. 'To suffer with all, to love with all, to be adequate to all demands and cries for help; to reach Nirvana and yet never to leave the four-ale bar, on this path what can one say but "It is known"?'

Many realized that the knower is above the fight. 'The Master within does not grovel in a Lower Self any more than he becomes ecstatic in a Higher Self. He lives in the situation, and becomes the situation, knowing the Suchness of the occasion.' We must end with a remark which lifts the whole subject to where it belongs. 'The "lower self" knows. That's why it fights. The Self, serene, untouched because It has no axe to grind, only smiles, because it accepts all phenomena without choice or distinction. It does not destroy; It never kills, even Its lower self, for the seeds of destruction are not in It. Only that which is of the nature of destruction can destroy or be destroyed. . . .'

Question 2. If good and evil are a pair of opposites, what keeps you good?
Again, the implied statement was at once challenged. 'Surely "If" is the operative word. I don't think good and evil are opposites. They are only terms applied to relative selfishness.' Another develops this. 'The terms are meaningless on their own.' Another lifts to the higher Third implicit in all duality. 'There is no opposite to true good. What we call good as an opposite to evil is perfection minus something; it is God descended into a manifestation perceptible to us limited beings; therefore it is not the Good. The Good is unlimited, God unlimited, Nirvana. . . .' As others showed, it is the false notion of duality which keeps the illusion alive. 'Why hang on to such pairs of opposites? Just live in Suchness, which knows neither.' And again, 'Evil and good are not reality, only comments, and now there are no reactions to comment upon. Yet there must be both if there is either.' One writer wrote in answer, 'Evil. Fortunately for Nirvana there is Samsara!' Several pointed out that we create the alleged problem by 'choosing'. 'The true Path has no difficulties until we make them by choosing—this is *good*, this is *evil*, for *me*.' As another crushingly

quoted from that classic, 'On Trust in the Heart', 'The conflict between right and wrong is the sickness of the mind'. Another disagreed. 'Tao cannot act save in a field of action. The opposites provide that field. We are Tao in action. Our purpose is not to be good but to be whole, so that all our vehicles can be in harmony with Tao.' Others took their stand in this Wholeness. 'There is no you to be *kept* good. I AM.'

Many wrote that the illusion of two is best resolved in right action. What matters, they agreed, is the thing to be done. And the motive should be compassion. 'What keeps one good is what keeps one evil, division, tension, lack of compassion. A heart filled with compassion would not consider good and evil, but would flow out in all directions, unjudging, uncondemning.'

Two more should be quoted. 'The lower self possesses all the virtues, bless it, and there is no merit whatsoever in being enlightened; to keep me good is to keep me ignorant.' Finally, a genuine 'pop-out'. 'Let us walk through the mist to the top of the hill. There is no view, but when the sun shines through there will be no mist.'

> *Question 3. Master and pupil walked to a nearby hill to watch the sunset. After a while the pupil murmured, 'So much beauty soon to be swallowed into night'. Said the master, 'So much beauty'. In a while it was dark. 'Alas, alas,' said the pupil sadly. Said the master, 'So much beauty'. It came on to rain. 'Let us go home', said the pupil. 'Yes', said the master, 'Let us go home. Will the sun be setting there?' Well?*

This proved the most difficult. Perhaps it was a poor question. There was much of the sunset (or sunrise) going on all the time, and the hill being home. 'Sunset, sunrise; the rain falls, the mists rise. Home is where we are. "Every day is a good day".' 'Starting is finishing; finishing is starting. There is no gap between the two ideas unless we put one there.' 'When they reached home it was raining hard *and* it was a dark night *and* the light of the setting sun rayed its glory on them as they stood on the nearby hill.' I think that many 'got' it. It was the comment on the experience that was difficult. One gave an interesting cause for the illusion of duality. 'In the eyesight of the mind there may be the sorrow of the setting sun, while the vision of the heart sees sunrise. Would this be because while the mind can only look, the heart can sometimes "see"?' Certainly the Zen 'seeing' is important. 'The knowledge and pattern of the whole of Reality is seen by looking fully at any part'—whether sunrise or sunset. A more Zen answer was the following. 'The path is slippery,' replied the pupil, 'but you do not need a light.' More classic, however, was this:

'Still seeing the sunset—again seeing the sunset.
No longer seeing the sunset—it has never left us.
Going home—will the sunset be there?
   True, that is the question!
Have a cup of tea!'
                Which leads one—where?

Question 4. Master and pupil waited for a bus. A bus arrived: it was full and went on. 'There'll be another soon', said the pupil. Said the master, 'There will be no more'. 'But I know there will', said the pupil. 'Fool!' said the master, hitting him over the head with his brolly. 'Oh,' said the pupil. 'I see what you mean. The road is wide indeed.' 'That's better', said the master, as another bus arrived. Which bus did they get into?

Here the whole Class spread themselves. 'There is only one bus to catch, the one right here, NOW. There is only one bus to miss, and where else could that be than right here, NOW?' 'They caught the bus that did not run because it was already there. Only the bus that does not run dare we catch, for if we leave Home for an instant we return to find the visiting card on the mat. Oh, why didn't we stay HERE?' A third put it more succinctly. 'Bus, Bus, Bus, Not Two. Total-mind-bus. No bus, Not-two buses. . . .'

One made an omnibus of Zen. 'Zen could be called an omnibus if taken as "the grinding of the void to dust"(?) . . . Of course there are no others; they could only get into the one they entered. It is always, "This is it." Hop on quick, quick. Can't change from Now. . . .' Another seems to have got on. 'How cold the hand-rail is, and how warm the inside! The fare? Yes, that must be paid, but after all it takes us home.' Several took the hint that the road is wide indeed. This is the third dimension method of cracking an either-or. How climb a ladder when it stops? By stepping sideways. Why study the road this way and that for buses? Cross it. 'Neither bus', wrote one. 'The road became wider and wider until it merged into the Void.' 'The whole universe, the past and future are encompassed in this wide, wide road. Walking home, the two ride in the empty bus which is full.' But the same writer gave a second answer and found them standing in the queue. The writer adds, 'Zen does not deliver us from the conditions of manifestation; it enables us to deal with them efficiently', which is worth remembering. One answer was accepted as blinding in its intensity, when read to the Class, but the writer confessed to its being a quotation. 'Did they go by bus at all? The way is wide enough for buses, cars, bicycles, even pedestrians.' On the other hand, 'There is a goal but no way. What we call way is our hesitation.'

I must end with something too lovely to be lost. One writer at least knows well the classic of English Zen—*Alice in Wonderland*. 'When Alice heard the observation, "there are plenty more", she said:

"I know things are much of a muchness, and I've heard of Suchness, so I suppose there must be a bus-ness.

"But how to get into a bus-ness? I could become a bus, I suppose . . . or would the bus be in me? Oh dear, now there aren't two of us any more, and I begin to feel as though I'm expanding. At this rate I shall never get into the bus that isn't coming."

"Dear me, why here is a bus-ness, and looking just like a bus too. I wonder if it's going our way . . . that is, if we have a way to go to. I'm really getting very confused."

"Make up your minds—that is, if you've got any." said the conductor sharply. "We're here now, and this is it." '

Any further comment must be yours.

An Approach to the Situation

We are faced with situations, grave and trivial, throughout the day. Assume one such arising suddenly, which is serious, needing all one's strength and wisdom, where the decision must be made on one's own responsibility alone.

With what in mind should one face the situation? It is suggested that the would-be man of Zen should train his mind to apply, immediately, a compound of the following principles.

It isn't there

1. The situation does not exist. Nor do I. All in manifestation, every thing that is, is *maya*, illusion, devoid alike of permanent qualities or total being.

If this can be seen as true, no situation is of more importance than a rapidly changing group of factors in a relative field of unreality! Meanwhile we must cope and rightly cope with the situation as we see it.

It is my karma. Therefore I cope

2. The whole complex of factors, and the I that faces it, is the collective result of a thousand million causes. It is the product of Karma, and having come to me is part of *my* karma. I made it so and I must therefore accept it utterly and cope with it faithfully.

It is all right

3. As the situation developed by the operation of universal law it is, in the proper meaning of the word, right. Indeed the universe would burst into pieces were any factor other than it is. It is indeed *all right*, just as everything else in existence is *all right*.

Only when these three truths have been assimilated and applied does the 'I' factor appear in relation to the situation.

Who faces it?

4. I ask myself who, or what aspect of the I (subject) is facing the situation (object)?

Can I see that all three factors in the situation, I, it, and the relation between them, are alike the product of 'my mind', which is an aspect of all-Mind, which is Buddha-Mind? Seeing this can I deliberately raise consciousness so that from a high level of 'my mind' I can cope with the situation, not in terms of my self, but as a conscious channel of the force of the 'Unborn', the Buddha-Mind within? Can I, in brief, get out of the way?

I must be impersonal

5. To the extent that I succeed in this I can be impersonal in deciding the right thing to be done. This excludes the voice of the lower self or ego, with its blind desire to be separate from and superior to other forms of the same Life-force. If I can extract from the total problem the desires of 'I' the tension in the problem will be largely gone.

Control of Response

6. Having raised the mind to remain impersonal I can the better control my response to the situation, of approval or disapproval, fear, regret, excitement or despair. Can I approach the ideal set out in the Bhagavad Gita; 'a constant, unwavering steadiness of heart upon the arrival of every event, whether favourable or unfavourable'? This is needful, for in the absence of such control it will be difficult to see just what, if anything, should be done.

Awareness of Non-duality

7. Finally, to come full circle, I must face the situation in terms of Non-duality ('Not one, not two'), for 'all distinctions are falsely imagined'. I am not different from nor other than the situation. We are parts of one another, for both of us are *sunyata*, devoid of measurable existence. There is nothing here but the coming together of facts and forces in respect of which I, for the moment, am. Nevertheless, if I see that here, in the unreality of everyday, there is something to be done which I should do, I do it, without thought, or motive, or the least concept of reward.

Ideally, these seven blend in one immediate response. Meanwhile, deep thought on each may serve to produce a new and nobler habit of mind; of 'right' response which, in the absence of self, will have no karmic effect, will 'leave no trace' of 'a mind abiding nowhere', in a world in which 'from the first not a thing is'. Neither the situation nor I nor the absence of either!

Only then shall we be free to laugh at all of them, wide, happy laughter, and in this joyous, deep content, 'walk on'—to the next situation.

'An Approach to the Situation'

'An Approach to the Situation' proved very helpful to the Zen Class, and on the second round was studied in conjunction with R. H. Blyth's translation of the forty-eight Zen stories in the *Mumonkan* (*Zen and Zen Classics* volume IV). The latter tested our Zen experience; the former gave ways of applying it.

Of course it is not suggested that being faced with a new and urgent situation we produce a copy of the 'Approach' and study its provisions before further action. But study, discussion and deep thought on its principles does, we find, produce a new ability to cope with the situation more speedily, efficiently and impersonally than before, and more and more in the spirit of Zen.

There is little to add to the Principles as originally formulated save a few quotations, and comments on the way in which the Class received them.

1. 'It isn't there'

Strangely enough, some Members found this not only the most helpful but the easiest to achieve. The basis for the statement of fact appears in Chapter 7, on 'The Wisdom which has gone Beyond', and can be studied in depth at pp. 114–15 of Dr Suzuki's *Studies in the Lankavatara Sutra*, where he says in terms, 'the Mahayana does not admit the existence of an external world; whatever qualities we think as belonging to the latter are creations or constructions of our own mind'. The subjective equivalent of this is to be found in the opening stanzas of the Dhammapada, to the effect that 'all that we are is the result of what we have thought'. In actual life it is possible to practise a with·drawal from involvement in these unreal things and circumstances, and while playing one's proper part in events to be more and more efficient without inner serenity being disturbed.

2. 'Anyhow, it's my karma'

The twin doctrines of Karma and Rebirth, basic to all schools of Buddhism, are least emphasized in that of Zen and for good reason. Karma is the cosmic law of compensation for each disturbance of the universal harmony. That which disturbs must restore the disturbance, but the disturbing factor is 'of the earth earthy', a self, a child of duality functioning in a world of relativity. As Zen training aims to destroy the very idea of such a separate self it is little concerned with its problems and suffering. The same applies to Rebirth. Whether the long preparation for Satori is crowned in this life or the next is of little consequence; what matters is the intensive preparation here and now. Meanwhile, in the words of the master Ryokwan, 'I follow my Karma as it moves, with perfect contentment'.

3. 'It's all Right'

Some find this very difficult, confusing right and Right. Of course very little is right in this present world, where the 'three fires' of hatred, lust and illusion burn so brightly, but every part of it, and the whole of it is Right.

The loveliest poem in Buddhist literature, 'On Trust in the Heart' by the second Patriarch, Seng-tsan, is full of this great truth. Read R. H. Blyth's analysis of the poem in Volume One of his *Zen and Zen Classics*, where he quotes from another poem,

> Just get rid of the mind that thinks
> 'This is good, this is bad',
> And without any special effort
> Wherever we live is good to live in.

'We must learn', he says 'to want what the universe wants, in the way it wants it, in that place, at that time.' More briefly, from the New Testament, 'Thy will be done'. More mystically, we must make way for 'Being's awareness of Itself in us'. Or Thoreau's words again, 'I know that the enterprise is worthy. I know that things work well. I have heard no bad news.' All this is surely what Unmon meant by his famous saying, 'Every day is a good day', and during it we shall meet with good and evil, truth and falsehood, pleasure and pain and, as Kipling said of triumph and disaster, 'treat those two impostors just the same'. So Browning, with the change of one letter, was right after all. 'God's in his heaven. All's Right with the World!'

4. 'Who am I that face the situation?'

Anatta is a matter of experience and not of doctrine, as Dr Suzuki many times pointed out. That the self is manifold is surely beyond argument. As Miss Horner has made clear from a dozen quotations, even in the Pali Canon at least two selves are admitted, and for myself I find the threefold division of St Paul, 'body, soul and spirit', helpful and true. The animal must be controlled. Looking at the five *skandhas*, constituents of the personality, the Buddha said, 'This is not mine; not this am I; herein is not the self of me'. Character, the 'soul' or Self, the reincarnating and ever-changing bundle of characteristics born under the sway of Karma, must be developed, purified, expanded until the level of consciousness is raised to see the situation from above, when the problem is seen to be, like all else, a product of the mind and as such, in the words of Hui-Neng, 'falsely imagined'. And above body and soul is THAT, the Unborn, Unconditioned which is not yours or mine. Truly the time comes when it matters not whether one aims at consciousness of the Full (Atman) or of the awareness of the Void which is Anatman. In either case the result is a foretaste of the Absolute, that nothing exists save Buddha-Mind, and from this Wisdom Compassion is born for all that lives in the sad field of duality.

5. 'I must be impersonal'

In the Chinese classic, *The Secret of the Golden Flower*, given to the West by Richard Wilhelm with the memorable Commentary by Carl Jung, we read: 'When occupations come to us we must understand them from the ground up. . . . When in ordinary life one has the ability always to react to things by reflexes only, without any admixture of a thought of others or of oneself, that is a circulation of the Light arising out of circumstances. It is the first secret.' This is not easy for most of us, who function normally at the level of *kama-manas*, thought entangled in desire. Yet until we lift to the level where the light of the intuition can illumine thought we shall not move upon the Way.

6. 'I must control response'

Here the Class achieved considerable success. All gimmicks and games are here permissible, and many made headway along the lines of No. 5 by success in No. 6. Some followed the advice in Chapter LXIV of the *Tao Te Ching*.

> Deal with a thing before it comes into existence.
> Regulate a thing before it gets into confusion.

It is the speed of right reaction or, as it is better put, response, which is now important. There is often a rush of memory, thought, feeling and some emotion. 'Drop the lot' seems the best advice; take a few deep breaths and then consider the situation calmly and objectively.

7. 'I know I am not One nor Two'

Here is the whole process speeded up. Thought moves so fast it merges in spontaneity. As Gai Eaton put it in *The Richest Vein*, 'Thought is not permitted to intervene between stimulus and reaction. An almost unimaginable spontaneity is demanded of the exponent of Zen. No second thoughts are allowed, not even first thoughts; only the most complete immediacy.' Here is direct action as distinct from ego-action. Now Being speaks and we obey. Now, reckless of result to self, all motive shed, we truly ceaselessly 'Walk On'. The Path is the Goal. The situation is ourselves. Now indeed we can and do laugh heartily.

Conclusion

So much for the problem, and a suggested alternative to the traditional training of the Rinzai School of Japan. Needless to say the course, which on the second run-through in the Zen Class lasted seven months, is but a brief synopsis of a training which for most of us will need many years and, as I believe, many lives for full accomplishment.

The distinction between the classical method and the suggested new is admittedly profound. The Japanese training paralyses thinking by the use of the koan, and liberates the whole strength of the mind to see directly into the Buddha-Mind within. But the koan, as already explained, cannot be effectively used in the absence of a qualified teacher, and that is why we are seeking, and here suggesting, an alternative.

Instead of by-passing and despising the intellect as of any service on the way to Satori, we have here accepted it as the natural and most efficient means for the Western mind to make its first approach. We have suggested a system of self-training which adopts it, learns to control it and raises it, in the sense of using it from a raised level of consciousness, until it functions freely on the plane of 'Illumined Thought'. Here, where the intuition is accepted as the sole faculty for *direct* vision of Reality, we develop it as far as we can—and wait.

In due course the first 'moment' arrives. We in the West must learn to identify it, to understand its significance and to adjust our whole being to its coming. This involves, first, that we apply the new-found enlightenment to every act and situation of the day, and secondly, that we become impersonal conduit-pipes for the Wisdom/Compassion/Light which has flooded our all too human mind.

First, we must learn to apply. In the West philosophers and the like write much of their discoveries; it does not occur to them to test them in the crucible of the market-place and office. Indeed, they are solemnly taught to remain 'objective' to their study, and to abstain from subjective involvement. Such a man is judged, says Dr Conze, himself a notable exception despised by some of his colleagues as such, 'by the consistency of his views, not with his life but with themselves', his other views. While preaching the doctrine of Anatta, for example, he makes no attempt to live as if he had no separate self. While proclaiming the need of universal love in the field of ethics he does not cease to hate his neighbour, and sees no reason why he should. The truth of Zen is otherwise. In the letter from Alan Watts already quoted he tells of the teaching of Sasaki Roshi. 'Zen, for instance, is a preparation for life in the world, not the goal of life in the world, and in its *highest* stages involves the study of sociology, politics, economics, etc.' Surely this must be so. For these are so many facets of Zen itself in action, and we are concerned with 'following our karma as it moves', in every place and time and situation. Satori is indeed the beginning of the Zen life and not its goal. From now on we are individuals dedicated to the service of the One Life of which we see all beings and ourselves as so many forms.

And secondly, we must learn to live as outposts of the Buddha-Mind which to an infinitesimal degree has suddenly lighted our own. We now see with increasing clarity that Father Merton was right, that 'Zen insight is not our awareness but Being's awareness of itself in us'. Here is the quintessence of mysticism and the heart of Zen. We are no longer confined within the ambit of our own past karma, but each mind is now alive with cosmic significance. Here is opportunity all but limitless to be one of the spiritual leaders of mankind, and we are face to face with a new duty, frightening and immense, and with grave dangers of its own. We must teach. Just how, to whom and when is a large subject, but here are points for consideration on a subject which can no longer be ignored.

We have a duty to share with others such spiritual truths as have come to us by way of direct experience, to the extent that those who are offered them seem to have need of them, are able to receive them and use them wisely. The range of give and take will extend from the Indian guru-chela relationship between a single pupil and his master to that described by the Master K. H. to A. P. Sinnett, who wrote to him of 'our prime duty of gaining knowledge and disseminating through all available channels such fragments as mankind in the mass may be ready to assimilate'. Between these limits there is the sowing of seed in a limited field, the offering of help to individuals who seem to need some specific help, the answering of appeals for help in this field and, needing the most care of all, the seeking out of those we feel would benefit by what we have to offer.

All these methods lie within the complementary pair of opposites of a duty to teach and a duty not to interfere in the spiritual progress of a fellow being. On the one hand there is the mandate in *The Voice of the Silence*, 'Point out the Way, however dimly and lost among the host as does the evening star to those who tread their way in darkness'. As against this, we read in the *Bhagavad Gita* that 'there is danger in another's duty', and the habit of interference is one of the worst of the Western mind. For knowledge is power, and spiritual knowledge is power of very high potency. To misuse it is hell and to be party to another's misuse of it has nearly the same result. In either case the would-be teacher is karmically responsible for all results. This is why the Hindu guru is loath to broadcast what he knows, and tests the pupil severely before handing on the least fragment of his own experience. The rightness of this attitude is proved by our knowledge of the opposite practice in the West, an indiscriminate publication to the world of little understood and deeply occult laws of nature. All who from evil motives or sheer ignorance—and the Law is indifferent to which—use them wrongly reap appalling damage. The misuse of splitting the atom, the evilly twisted application of ESP, brain-washing and much more, all these follow, and judging by present Western morality or the lack of it, much more is yet to come.

What shall we teach? 'Those who have realized the Essence of Mind', says Hui-Neng, 'give suitable answers according to the temperament of the enquirer.' At most, it has been frivolously said, one should teach at a level a trifle higher than the easy capacity of the pupil, to make him jump for it as a dog for a bone.

The teacher must allow the pupil to make mistakes and to suffer seriously for them. Only thus will he learn. There are no utterly right methods of learning or of teaching and in the end all methods are left behind. Meanwhile dogma, of doctrine or method, robs the pupil of his right to choose for himself and to earn and learn from the karma thereby caused.

The teacher must have clean hands. He must be humble of mind in the art of passing on, not letting a sense of I be present in the teaching but letting IT teach what IT will. He therefore has no pride in success and makes no claims at all.

Why? Because in truth he has nothing to teach, and none can take ought from him. He can but point the Way—'even Buddhas do but point the Way'—and at most, as Dr Suzuki once told us, bring back into the right direction the efforts of those who for the moment seem to have lost it. The teacher stimulates and provokes effort. His aim is ever to make the pupil 'work out his own salvation', as were the Buddha's dying words. As P. G. Bowen records the profound teaching

N   193 of the Berber philosopher Mehlo Moya, 'If thou would feed the hungry teach them to sow, for no man reaps what another sows in the Garden of the King'.

While encouraging the study of literature of intuitive inspiration, as in the noblest scriptures of mankind, he reduces discussion and eliminates argument completely. For these are of the intellect, and the experience sought lies ever beyond it. He is concerned to rouse intuitive awareness, and whatever the 'skilful means' invoked to this end, of scriptures, sermons, silence or even blows, he will teach in the end, if at all, by what he is rather than by what he does or says. In Emerson's famous words, 'What you are speaks so loudly I cannot hear what you say'.

For the teacher's task is to reveal the Buddha-Mind now wakening in the pupil's mind. As Dr Suzuki makes clear in a hitherto unpublished manuscript, 'we must attain the Unattainable in an unattainable way'.

This means of course that the teacher is really teaching Nothing, Emptiness, the Void, the Void within himself which is the universal consciousness. But not as such. As Hui-Neng says, 'In the functioning of the Essence of Mind and in conversation with others, outwardly we should free ourselves from attachment to objects, and inwardly we should free ourselves from attachment to the idea of the Void'. In this high duty he will be indifferent to the pupil's expressed needs, for the latter will have no good knowledge of what is best for him. He will be rude if need be, turn the enquirer away, deliberately increase existing difficulties, all to raise still higher the internal tension and 'head of steam' needful for the actual break-through to some measure of enlightenment. This is the traditional Zen way, and it serves to prevent the pupil leaning on the teacher, to the point of what psychologists in the West call a mental transference difficult to disentangle.

In brief, he must be scrupulous in non-interference, leaving the pupil to find for himself his own best way to the common end, for 'the ways to the One are as many as the lives of men', as I was taught some fifty years ago, and each must tread his own.

And the pupil? He must prepare himself for such help as the teacher of his choice may give. 'When the pupil is ready the master appears.' He will ask questions but learn, as Blyth puts it, that 'the real answer to any question is the question really understood'. For in Zen the question and answer are seen as another of the pairs of opposites. He will admit no authority for any teaching and be ready to criticize all teaching given. Such is the Zen way, for in a relative world nothing is true until found to be true by the individual's intuitive perception. But he must rise or attempt to rise to the level of the teaching given and there receive it, for any attempt to drag it down to the plane of argument reduces Zen experience to the level of concept, in which there is no Zen.

Does all this set so high a standard that none will dare to teach? This is fear not wisdom, for we learn by teaching, and some say that we learn in no other way. Learning, teaching, these are one, in the shrine-room, office or the home.

Finally, the Zen-seeker must break himself of the habit, to which most of us are deeply conditioned, of setting aside special times for 'Buddhism' and 'Zen', and devoting all other times to family, business and social life. As Dr Suzuki quotes the master Pen-hsien, 'If you really wish to get into the truth of Zen, get it while walking, while standing, while sleeping or sitting, while talking or remaining silent, or while engaged in all kinds of daily work.' The central theme of all our thinking must be at all times and in all places the Unthinkable. This is upmost in the mind unless some other duty presses to its momentary exclusion. As Daito Kokushi admonished his pupils, 'Be ever mindful throughout the day to apply yourselves to the study of the Unthinkable. Time passes like an arrow; never let your minds be disturbed by worldly cares. Ever be on the look-out. O monks, be diligent, be diligent!'

Only thus, with sustained, enormous effort does the pupil-mind regain its own enlightenment or, more truly, allow the Unborn Buddha-Mind to manifest through this particular aspect of Itself. Carl Jung of Zürich, surely one of the greatest minds of Europe in the twentieth century, was echoing a basic truth of Buddhism when he insisted, in volume after volume, on the paramount importance of the individual. 'A concept', he says in *Essays on Contemporary Events*, 'is not a carrier of life. The sole and natural carrier of life is the individual.' The council, the company, the State itself are but collections of men and women, and as entities are but concepts invented by the individual mind. 'After all,' Jung enquires, 'who is the State? It is the agglomeration of all the nonentities of which it is made up. If it could be personified the result would be an individual, a monster, which would be intellectually and ethically on a far lower level than most of the individuals of which it is composed, for it represents mass psychology raised to the highest power.' And he quotes, in a footnote to page 31, from Pestalozzi's *Ideen* a notable passage: 'Our race develops its human qualities in essence only from face to face, from heart to heart. It can do this only in small circles, which gradually grow larger in the warmth of feeling and love, and in trust and confidence. All the means requisite for the education of man are the concern of the individual.'

The advancement of the human race will come from an increasing number of individuals climbing the mountain path to self-enlightenment. No pact or treaty affects the minds of men or alters character. So long as the individual is in tension between the demands of its lower, selfish qualities and the vision, waking slowly, of the God within, so long will that individual be at war within, and project his inner strife into the world without in class war, trade war, national and world war.

'Work out your own salvation with diligence', said the Buddha, and he was speaking in these dying words to the men about him individually. Such is the Buddha-Way, a long hard road for everyman for years and lives to come. There will be full enlightenment and peace on earth when all men are enlightened, not before. Meanwhile the individual, his whole life dedicated to this end, can only 'walk on' as he may, knowing that above him on the mountain path are a thousand hands to help him, and below, a million hands that need his own.

To this end this course is dedicated. May it serve.

Suggested Minimum Library for the Course

Chosen from books at present in print. For the use of students who are prepared to study deeply with a view to intuitive understanding.

Zen Buddhism, and *Zen, A Way of Life.* Both by Christmas Humphreys. To put Zen Buddhism in the field of Buddhism.

Selected Sayings from the Perfection of Wisdom, by Dr E. Conze. To understand the philosophy behind Zen.

Buddhist Wisdom Books, by Dr E. Conze, (volume one). The Diamond and Heart Sutras unfolded.

Dr Suzuki's own *Introduction to Zen Buddhism.*

The Sutra of Hui-Neng, and Dr Suzuki's *The Zen Doctrine of No-Mind,* which is a commentary upon it.

The Zen Teaching of Huang Po. With Hui-Neng, the two basic books of Ch'an-Zen scriptures.

R. H. Blyth's *Zen in English Literature.* A most helpful work on Zen for the Western Mind.

R. H. Blyth's *'Mumonkan', the Gateless Gate.* (*Zen and Zen Classics,* Vol. IV). 48 Mondo for deep digestion.

Dr Suzuki's *Essays in Zen Buddhism,* Series I, and *The Field of Zen.*

The Zen Revival. Thomas Merton. A powerful essay by a great Catholic mystic.

For reference and as a Bedside Book, *The Wisdom of Buddhism.* An anthology by Christmas Humphreys.

Other Reading at choice: The *Tao Te Ching;* The *Dhammapada;* The *Bhagavad Gita; The Fourth Gospel; The Voice of the Silence,* trans. by H. P. Blavatsky.

Brief Glossary

Sk = Sanskrit, P = Pali, Chin = Chinese, Jap = Japanese

ANATTA (P). The essentially Buddhist doctrine of non-ego.

ATMAN (Sk). The Supreme Self; Universal Consciousness.

AVIDYA (Sk). Ignorance; lack of enlightenment.

BHAKTI (Sk). Devotion to a spiritual ideal.

BHAVANA (Sk & P). Self-development by any means, but especially by the method of mind-control, concentration and meditation.

BODHISATTVA (Sk). One whose 'being' or 'essence' (*sattva*) is *Bodhi*. The Wisdom resulting from direct perception of Truth, with the compassion awakened thereby.

BRAHMAN. The impersonal and supreme Principal of the Universe.

BUDDHA. A title meaning Awakened, in the sense of Enlightened. The founder of Buddhism in the sixth century B.C.

BUDDHI (Sk). The vehicle of Enlightenment (Bodhi). The faculty of direct awareness of Reality. The intuition.

DHARMA (Sk), DHAMMA (P). System, doctrine, law, truth, cosmic order (according to the context). The Buddhist Teaching.

DHYANA (Sk). Meditation. A stage on the way to Prajna (q.v.). The Japanese derivation of the word is ZEN which, however, has a very different meaning.

DUKKHA (P). Suffering, in any form and from whatever cause. In the Theravada those forms mostly arising from selfish desire. In the Mahayana, arising from manifestation itself as being in duality whereas the ultimate Truth lies in Non-duality.

KAMA (Sk). Desire of the senses, especially sexual desire. The craving which arises from the false belief in an ego or self separate from the rest of manifestation.

KARMA (Sk). The Law of cause and effect, as applied to the mind. Karma is not limited by time and space, and is not strictly individual; there is group Karma, family, national etc. The doctrine of Rebirth is an essential corollary to that of Karma.

KARUNA (Sk). Active compassion, cf. *prajna*.

KOAN (Jap). A word or phrase creating a problem that cannot be solved by reasoning or thought. An exercise, used in Rinzai Zen Buddhism, and to a less extent in the Soto school, for breaking the limitations of thought and developing the intuition.

198

MAHAYANA. The Buddhist School of the Great Vehicle (of liberation); also called the Northern School (Tibet, Mongolia, China, Korea and Japan).

MANAS (Sk). Mind. The rational faculty in man.

MAYA (Sk). Illusion, and popularly used in this sense. Philosophically, the phenomenal universe, being subject to differentiation and impermanence is Maya.

NIRVANA (Sk). The supreme goal of Buddhist endeavour; release from the limitations of separate existence. A state attainable in this life. One who has attained to this state is called *arhat*.

PALI. One of the early languages of Buddhism. It was later adopted by the Theravadins as the language in which to preserve the memorized teachings of the Buddha.

PRAJNA (Sk). Transcendental Wisdom. One of the *paramitas*. One of the two pillars of the Mahayana, the other being *karuna* (compassion).

SAMADHI. Contemplation on Reality. The eighth step on the Eightfold Path.

SAMKHARAS (P). Mental predispositions; the karmic results of mental illusion. One of the five *skandhas*.

SAMSARA (Sk & P). Continued 'coming-to-be'. Existence in the world as compared with Nirvana.

SATORI (Jap). The 'goal' of Zen Buddhism. A state of consciousness beyond the plane of discrimination and differentiation.

SILA (Sk & P). The Buddhist code of morality.

SKANDHA (Sk). The five causally-conditioned elements of existence forming a being or entity. They are inherent in every form of life, either in an active or a potential state.

SUNYATA (Sk). Voidness. The doctrine that asserts the Voidness of Ultimate Reality. It abolishes all concepts of dualism and proclaims the essential oneness of the phenomenal and the noumenal.

TAO (Chin). The central concept of Taoism, as expressed in the *Tao Te Ching*. Can mean the One and the Way to it.

THERAVADA (P). The 'Doctrine of the Elders' who formed the first Buddhist Council. The School of Buddhism of Ceylon, Burma and Thailand.

TRISHNA (Sk). (In P. Tanha.) Thirst for sentient existence; separative desire.

VEDANA (P). Sense reaction to contact. The seventh link in the twelve nidanas, the chain of causation, producing the craving of thirst for existence.

VIJNANA (Sk). Consciousness; the faculty by which one cognizes the phenomenal world.

ZEN (Jap). A corruption of the Chinese *Ch'an* which in turn is derived from the Sanskrit *Dhyana*. The School of Zen Buddhism which passed from China to Japan in the thirteenth to fourteenth centuries.

Index

QUEST BOOKS
are published by
The Theosophical Society in America,
Wheaton, Illinois 60189-0270,
a branch of a world fellowship,
a membership organization
dedicated to the promotion of the unity
of humanity and the encouragement of the study
of religion, philosophy, and science, to the end that
we may better understand ourselves and our place
in the universe. The Society stands for complete
freedom of individual search and belief.
For further information about its activities,
write, call 1-800-669-1571,
e-mail olcott@theosophia.org,
or consult its Web page:
http://www.theosophical.org

*The Theosophical Publishing House
is aided by the generous support of
THE KERN FOUNDATION,
a trust established by Herbert A. Kern
and dedicated to Theosophical education.*